Endorsements

"After developing a long-term friendship with Wesley, I assumed I knew about all his struggles; however, upon reading his story, I learned so much more about how God can work in a person's life. *The Blueprint of Becoming* renews my spirit and my hope in God's ability to remove my shortcomings."

—Justin R.
Church Council Chairman

"This book was written to help you overcome your past failures and struggles. It will help you push forward in your walk with Christ. I found it to be well-written, and it provides readers with a practical understanding and perspective on pursuing Christ and the victory that can be experienced in Him. I highly recommend that you give this a read."

—Donna F.

"For anyone on a spiritual journey, whether searching the stars for meaning or exploring deeper truths, *The Blueprint of Becoming* offers a relatable companion. Wes shares his own path with honesty and insight, guiding readers toward discovering God in the midst of their search for purpose and direction."

—Joe W.
Celebrate Recovery Ministry Leader

"*The Blueprint of Becoming* is the most straightforward guide to navigating life and its challenges that I've read. You do not have to wade through a lot of fluff or hard to understand words and concepts; Wes cuts through that with his own personal story, a wealth of Bible verses and ideas that are extremely relatable, and simple tools to help you overcome the obstacles in your life and view who you are becoming with a new mindset. Wes's book will become a part of your support system, every bit as important as the people who surround you as you follow your path to becoming."

—**Joey Hawkins**
Pastor, Cedar Falls Christian Church

The
BLUEPRINT
of
BECOMING

*A Practical Guide to Faith, Failure, and
Finding Your Way Forward*

WESLEY FARNSWORTH

LUCIDBOOKS

The Blueprint of Becoming:
A Practical Guide to Faith, Failure, and Finding Your Way Forward

Copyright © 2025 Wesley Farnsworth

Published by Lucid Books in Houston, TX
www.LucidBooks.com

All rights reserved. No part of this publication may be reproduced, stored in a retrieval system, or transmitted in any form by any means, electronic, mechanical, photocopy, recording, or otherwise, without the prior permission of the publisher, except as provided for by USA copyright law.

Unless otherwise indicated, are taken from the Holy Bible, New International Version®, NIV®. Copyright ©1973, 1978, 1984, 2011 by Biblica, Inc.™ Used by permission of Zondervan. All rights reserved worldwide. www.zondervan.com The "NIV" and "New International Version" are trademarks registered in the United States Patent and Trademark Office by Biblica, Inc.™

Celebrate Recovery® is a Christ-centered 12-step recovery program and a registered trademark of Saddleback Church. This book is not affiliated with or endorsed by Celebrate Recovery® or Saddleback Church. References to the program reflect the author's personal experience and are used for testimonial and educational purposes only. More information can be found at celebraterecovery.com

eISBN: 978-1-63296-843-2
ISBN: 978-1-63296-842-5

For permissions or inquiries, contact:
Wesley@wesleyfarnsworth.com

Special Sales: Most Lucid Books titles are available in special quantity discounts. Custom imprinting or excerpting can also be done to fit special needs. Contact Lucid Books at Info@LucidBooks.com

*To my four amazing children,
may you always know that no matter where you start,
God has a beautiful plan for your life.
You are my greatest blessing and motivation.*

*Special thanks to everyone
who encouraged me to write,
who listened to my endless rambles about "my book,"
or who asked, "How's the book coming?"
Your belief in me made this possible.*

Contents

Introduction 1

Section 1
My Testimony

Chapter 1
Roots and Wings: Navigating Faith 9

Chapter 2
Breaking Chains: Confronting Co-Dependency,
Pornography, and Anger 17

Section 2
Biblical Perspectives

Chapter 3
The Power of Transformation in the Bible 29

Chapter 4
Understanding Your Current Stars – The Stars That
Shape Our Lives 37

Chapter 5
The Divine Blueprint: God's Design for Your Life 53

Section 3
Beginning to Change

Chapter 6
    Overcoming Obstacles and Adversities 73

Chapter 7
    Renewing Your Mind and Heart..83

Chapter 8
    Stepping into Your Transformed Future 91

Conclusion 99
Final Blessings...105
Epilogue: Becoming Never Ends..107
Scripture Index 109
Scripture Reference Table by Topic..115
About the Author 117
Additional Resources 119

Introduction

In 2019, I attended a Celebrate Recovery meeting where I heard a testimony that sparked a deep conversation about transformation with a group of men. In recovery, every conversation feels intentional. Even the simplest stories can reveal powerful truths about healing and transformation. That night, God brought to my mind a recurring theme I had encountered in medieval-themed movies: the idea of "changing your stars."

That night, a particular scene from the movie *A Knight's Tale* began playing in my head as we talked about the testimony. In the scene, a young peasant boy watches as knights parade down the street, sitting atop their horses full of confidence, armor gleaming, and banners flying high. In awe, he turns to his father and asks if he could one day be like them, a knight, someone noble, respected, and free. His father reassures him that anything is possible, but before the boy can dream, another man nearby scoffs, telling him, "You can't change your stars." The words hung heavy, and the boy's facial expression changed as though seemingly sealing his fate.

Maybe you've felt that way too, like your future was already written in stone, defined by your past or what others said about you—like there was nothing you could do about it. I know I have.

That scene resonated with me because I felt like that for much of my life. I believed the lie that my circumstances, shortcomings, and mistakes were immovable, fixed points in the constellation of my life. I lived under the weight of that lie, convinced I wasn't enough, and that real transformation was out of reach.

Growing up, I was shy and unsure of myself. I struggled to connect with others, often feeling inadequate and out of place. To survive socially, I became a chameleon, blending into whatever crowd I was in, laughing at jokes I didn't find funny, and keeping my true thoughts and feelings hidden.

The fear of rejection ran so deep that I didn't just hide who I was, I began to forget who I was. This wasn't limited to friendships; it bled into every area of my life, especially my relationships with the opposite sex.

I convinced myself I wasn't smart enough, attractive enough, or worthy enough to be loved as I truly was. The harder I worked to earn acceptance, the more disconnected I felt from my identity. The more I tried to conform to what others wanted, the more I became trapped.

I felt like the stars of my life were fixed, that my insecurities and failures were set in stone. The idea of "changing my stars" felt impossible, like that was something reserved for better, braver, or more "worthy" people. I believed the lie that my worth was tied to how others perceived me. I didn't yet understand that my true worth came from the One who created me.

But God, in His infinite patience and love, refused to let me stay stuck. Over the years, His truth began to pierce through the lies I had clung to for so long. It wasn't an overnight transformation but a slow and steady process. Through Scripture, prayer, and the encouragement of others, I began to see myself the way God sees me. One verse became an anchor for my soul:

Introduction

I praise you because I am fearfully and wonderfully made; your works are wonderful, I know that full well.

—Psalm 139:14

At first, these words felt foreign, almost too good to be true. Could it really be that I was "fearfully and wonderfully made"? Could it be that my worth didn't depend on my performance or approval from others?

But as I meditated on this truth, something shifted inside me. I began to realize that my value wasn't rooted in what I could achieve or how well I fit in. My value was fixed—unchanging—because it was rooted in the unshakable love of the God who created me.

This realization was both liberating and transformative. It gave me the courage to stop striving for approval and to live authentically. The "changing your stars" metaphor took on a whole new meaning.

It wasn't about becoming someone else to please others but about stepping into the person God created me to be. It was about realigning my life to reflect His purpose and design.

Our lives are like constellations, a breathtaking tapestry of moments, relationships, struggles, and triumphs. Each "star" represents a facet of our journey, guiding us through the vastness of existence.

Yet there are seasons when our constellations feel dimmed by shadows, circumstances that seem unchangeable, failures that feel unforgivable, and doubts that cloud our direction. But the good news is this: With God, no star is fixed beyond His power to realign. He invites us to step into His divine blueprint, to take hold of the promises He's spoken over us, and to walk in the freedom He designed for us.

This journey isn't always easy. It requires confronting the lies we've believed, letting go of our burdens, and trusting God to lead us into new and unfamiliar territory. There were moments in my journey when I doubted, stumbled, and fell back into old patterns. But even in my weakness, God remained faithful.

Again and again, He reminded me: It's not about perfection; it's about surrender. It's not about having it all together but trusting the One who does. It's about allowing Him to rewrite the narrative of our lives, one star at a time.

This book isn't just my testimony; it's also an invitation. An invitation to examine your own life, the patterns, struggles, and doubts that feel unchangeable, and consider what it might look like to hand them over to God.

Through the wisdom of Scripture and the power of faith, we'll explore what it means to embrace transformation and step into God's purpose for your life.

No matter where you are in your journey, I want you to know this: You are not defined by your past, your mistakes, or the opinions of others. You are defined by the God who created you, loves you, and calls you by name. With Him, transformation is always possible. Together, let's begin this journey of change, star by star, step by step, and discover the life of freedom, purpose, and grace that God has written into your design.

> *"Before I formed you in the womb I knew you, before you were born I set you apart; I appointed you as a prophet to the nations."*
>
> —Jeremiah 1:5

As I've walked this path, I've come to see the Bible not just as a source of comfort, but as a map—its truths like stars, guiding me when my direction felt lost. Exploring Scripture more deeply, I discovered powerful truths that were guideposts during my darkest seasons. These truths became my compass—and they might become yours too.

Introduction

Biblical Truths That Help Us Change Our Stars

As the North Star guides sailors, the Bible offers a constant light, guiding us through even the most uncertain nights. Like stars in the night sky, its truths help us find our way when everything feels uncertain.

- **Divine Design**: Just as the Creator fashioned the universe with intention, the Bible reveals that we are meticulously designed with purpose. The Bible, prayer, and our relationship with God give us a roadmap to uncover our unique destinies, guiding us to understand our roles in the grand narrative of existence.

- **Renewal and Regeneration**: Just as the stars emerge anew with each nightfall, biblical teachings advocate for the renewal of our minds and hearts. Through faith and adherence to scriptural truths, we shed old patterns and embrace new perspectives, paving the way for inner and outer transformation.

- **Forgiveness and Redemption**: The Bible recounts numerous stories of redemption and forgiveness, illustrating the potential for renewal even after moments of failure. This grace-infused concept invites us to release the weight of past mistakes, enabling us to chart a course toward a brighter constellation.

- **Guidance Amidst Uncertainty**: As ancient navigators trusted the stars to find their way, the Bible is our true North Star, offering wisdom when life feels uncertain. Its teachings provide clear moral guidance, helping us make choices that align with our values and propelling us toward positive change.

- **Community and Fellowship**: Just as constellations form patterns, the Bible emphasizes the importance of community and fellowship. Engaging with others who share a commitment to transformation provides mutual support, fostering an environment conducive to growth.

- **Eternal Hope**: The Bible's narratives of hope and restoration remind us that transformation is not bound by time. These stories encourage us to persevere through challenges, trusting that even in the darkest of nights, our stars can shine brightly again. Just as God brought light into my darkest moments, the Bible reminds us that no night is too dark for His redemption.

In the chapters ahead, we'll move from my personal journey to biblical stories of transformation and practical tools and reflections to help you navigate your journey of change.

Section 1

My Testimony

Before we can talk about change, we must talk about where we've been. This section is my story, raw, real, and sometimes hard to tell. But it also contains God's grace, mercy, and unshakable faithfulness.

I share it not to draw attention to myself, but to show what's possible when we surrender to the One who can truly transform us. As you read, my hope is that you find glimpses of your own story, feel less alone in your struggles, and begin to believe that your past doesn't have to define your future.

Chapter 1
Roots and Wings: Navigating Faith

In a Pastor's Home

Let me preface this by saying that my parents were, and still are, the most amazing people. Most of the feelings I carried were self-imposed.

But being a pastor's kid came with what felt like two sets of rules: the ones everyone else lived by, and the ones I believed I had to live by. Even when no one said it out loud, I felt like I had to be perfect. After all, I wasn't just representing myself, I was representing them, and by extension, God.

Growing Up in a Pastor's Home

My Dad was a full-time evangelist with the Assemblies of God who was always on the road preaching at whatever church would allow him to speak. My mom also worked in ministry, serving as the Women's Ministry director for the Assemblies of God in the State of Michigan for many years.

For those who are unfamiliar with the term, an evangelist is similar to a pastor except that they are not assigned to a single church. Evangelists travel to speak at various churches, and they are usually supported by the "love offerings" collected during their visit or by gifts from individuals.

Anyway, growing up, church was a constant. If the doors were open, it seemed as if we were there. It was the only place I had friends. During the week, neighborhood kids would come by and ask to play, but that was often with my brothers, rather than with me, unless they needed one more for a game.

As a result, I spent much of my time in my bedroom surfing the internet on my computer or watching TV once I was old enough and had saved enough money from my paper route to purchase one.

At church, I began serving at a young age. I started by helping with the overhead projector; yes, those were my fingers you saw moving the lyrics on and off the screen during worship service. After a while, I transitioned to working in the sound booth, ushering, serving as a greeter, and assisting my mom as she led the children's ministry.

I accepted Christ at a young age and was baptized in water at the local church camp around the age of seven or eight, if memory serves me correctly.

Because my dad was a pastor, my mom was a ministry director, and we always attended church, I thought that I knew everything there was to know about God. I knew to pray before meals and at bedtime and to ask God to heal people who were sick. I also knew that God was my friend and that He died for my sins. Essentially, I knew many Sunday school answers.

I remember one time during Vacation Bible School at my aunt's church, I got bored in class and decided to sit in the hall. When the teacher asked why I was bored and sitting there, I said, "Because I already know everything there is to know about God."

Now looking back, I know that my walk wasn't as rock-solid as I thought it was; in fact, I didn't know much at all at that time.

Over the years, though, as I've grown, God has done many things to show me just how much he loves me. Philippians 4:19 says, *"And my God will meet all your needs according to the riches of his glory in Christ Jesus."*

God Will Provide

Allow me to quickly share two defining moments that shaped who I am today.

The first lesson I learned is that God always provides for those who trust in him. Over the years, God has provided for my family many times. There were times when a check would arrive in our mailbox for the exact amount of a bill that was due. Other times, cards would arrive with a bit of extra cash, allowing us to do something fun that otherwise wouldn't have happened.

However, two specific events stand out in my mind that make Philippians 4:19 resonate with me in my spiritual life. The first of these events took place shortly after my dad became ill. Because of his illness, he was forced to stop working, and we instantly became a single-income family. In the weeks leading up to Christmas that year, my parents sat my siblings and me down and explained that money was tight due to everything that was going on, and they simply couldn't afford gifts that year.

This would be the first Christmas that there wouldn't be anything for us under the tree on Christmas morning. That news wasn't easy to give or take. Like all kids, I loved having things under the tree to rip open! But we knew what was happening and understood. We were determined to still make it a great Christmas.

But this is where the story gets interesting. You see, God was aware of what was happening. He knew our heart's desire. He put our family on the hearts of many pastors and churches across the State of Michigan, and unbeknownst to us, they began collecting gifts on our behalf.

One night, while enjoying some quality time as a family, we heard a knock at our front door. It was a local pastor who explained that he had a van full of gifts for us from some local churches. We unloaded his van, expressed our thanks, and he left. Shortly after that, we heard another knock, then another. That Christmas, my family had enough gifts for three or four Christmases.

That Christmas, I didn't just hear about God's provision; I experienced it firsthand in a very real and tangible way. He showed me that He takes care of those who follow Him and dedicate their lives to Him. That Christmas, the things I had heard repeatedly in church services began to make sense and take on new meaning in my personal life.

Another pivotal moment came several years later in 2004. My youngest brother, Stephen, who was sixteen, put his bike into the back of his car, said, "See ya later, Pops" to my Dad, and left to meet with and go riding with some friends. However, he wouldn't make it to that meetup because God called him home. To say that this was hard for my family and me is an understatement.

I can remember the day it happened like it was yesterday. I was playing on a softball team with my coworkers. We had just finished our game, and we were sitting in the grass behind the ball diamond, shooting the breeze, when we saw a cop pull into the parking lot.

Jokingly, all the guys began to say that the cop was there for me, and they asked what I had done. Of course, I went along with the joke and made something up. Little did I know . . . he really was there for me. As he walked over the grassy area where we were all sitting, he called out, "I'm looking for Wesley Farnsworth." I acknowledged him, and he said, "You need to get home; there has been a family emergency."

I immediately got up, grabbed my stuff, and ran to my car without missing a beat. I began thinking it was my grandmother who had passed because she had been ill. However, the more I thought about it, the less it made sense because I didn't believe they would dispatch a local cop for something like that. Would they?

When I got home, I found two of my friends sitting on the front step; I said hello as I pushed by them and proceeded up the steps and into the front door. Inside, I found my mom, dad, and brother huddled in tears on a single recliner chair. That's when I heard the words: "Stephen has been killed in a car accident."

This news rocked my world. How could my youngest brother be gone? I had just seen him earlier that day, and suddenly, he was gone. But it was through that tragedy that God continued to teach me.

As we began to plan the funeral and everything else that comes along with it, we began to pray and ask God for help because we honestly didn't have the money to pay for it. That's when God once again stepped in and seemed to say, "I got this!" God provided for us by covering not only the funeral in full but also all the extra costs, including the cost of the gravesite.

When it came time for the funeral service, I was blown away. We ended up with a standing-room-only service; in fact, many were unable to even enter the sanctuary where the service was held. Then there was the two-mile-long procession of cars to the graveside service, where at least three people were saved when given the chance.

But God wasn't done yet. When some families in our church heard what happened, they came together and purchased tickets for my family to accompany them on a cruise so that we could get away and reconnect as a family while finding our new "normal."

This was huge for me. Growing up, money was always tight, so we never got to take family vacations unless it was to a church where my dad would preach, and we would stay a few extra days. Most of the time, it was to St. Ignas, Michigan, where my Dad would speak at a church every summer. So, we would go along as a family, and while there, we would take a day to visit Mackinac Island and explore.

So, to have something like this happen on the heels of my brother's death struck a chord in my heart and reaffirmed how much God cares for me.

Bear with each other and forgive one another if any of you has a grievance against someone. Forgive as the Lord forgave you.

—Colossians 3:13

Forgiveness in the Face of Tragedy

This brings me to a second life lesson I learned from my parents. Let's go back to the night my brother died in a car accident. As I mentioned, that was a very emotional and trying time for me, let alone my parents.

You see, they had already lost one son shortly after birth, and here they were experiencing the loss of yet another child. As a father myself, I can't begin to imagine that pain, and I pray that it's not something I will ever experience. However, despite that pain, I learned another crucial lesson.

Shortly after I arrived home from the softball fields that day, the police came in to talk with us. They explained what had happened as best as they could. They explained that my brother's passenger-side tires had gone off the road as he was going around the bend of a curve in the road. When he tried to get back onto the road, he overcorrected, causing the car to end up sideways on the road. Usually, this would be okay, and the driver would be able to correct themselves and continue.

However, a cement truck was coming down the road in the opposite direction that day. As my brother's car went sideways due to him overcorrecting, the truck collided with his vehicle, killing him instantly.

Now I'm sure you're asking, "Why do I need to know this?" Simply put, it's an integral part of this life lesson. Forgiveness isn't easy for anyone, especially someone who has just lost a family member, let alone a child.

However, that night, as the officer stood in front of us, I heard my father ask to meet the truck driver involved in his son's accident. Of course, the officer informed us that this was not possible. However, it was at this moment that the life lesson truly took root. Despite the pain, my dad pushed his emotions aside for that moment and looked at that officer and said, "I understand, will you please deliver a message for me?"

He said, "Please tell the driver that what happened was not his fault, and that we, that I forgive him." This selfless act of forgiveness sent a compelling message to me. As I mentioned earlier, growing up, I always heard the Bible verses about forgiveness. But here, in the most painful and tragic moment I had ever experienced, I witnessed those verses put into action. That night, I learned precisely what it meant to forgive.

I'm sure you're wondering what this has to do with your recovery. Well, let me tell you. Because of moments like these—lessons wrapped in pain and provision—I've come to trust God's power over anything I face.

Chapter 2
Breaking Chains: Confronting Co-Dependency, Pornography, and Anger

Living to Please Everyone

Due to the nature of my parents' work, I often felt pressure to conform and be the perfect kid. The last thing I wanted was to make them look bad, so I became a master chameleon. I could blend into almost any environment and go pretty much anywhere.

But in trying to be everything for everyone, I lost sight of who I was. I began thinking about what others would think and say about my comments or opinions. So, I became good at judging others and adjusted what I said to be accepted by them. I didn't care about what I thought; I cared only about what they thought.

That need for approval affected more than just how I acted, it eventually began to shape what I pursued.

The Birth of an Addiction

It was also through this co-dependency that my addiction to pornography was born.

It began while out with friends one day, and they began talking and joking about a subject I knew nothing about. But I laughed and tried to play along to ensure that I fit in.

Later that night, when I got home, I began searching the internet for some of the terms I had heard, so I wouldn't be uninformed if they came up again. After all, it's much easier to fit in, when you don't have to pretend you know what is being talked about.

That night, those internet searches opened a door I didn't know how to close. What started as curiosity became a chain that followed me into adulthood. But remember, I was a master chameleon.

I was able to hide the addiction from anyone and everyone. Looking back, I can see how porn quietly wrecked things in my life, though I kept telling myself—like anyone with an addiction does—that it wasn't a problem because I could stop whenever I wanted.

The years from 2006 to 2008 were probably the lowest point in my life as far as these addictions are concerned. In 2006, I married a beautiful woman who was my best friend. But my porn addiction was strong, and it caused me to act wrongly and hurt her on many levels, for which I am and always will be sorry. A year later, in 2007, I joined the Air Force, and during my technical school training, my addiction ramped up even more.

As far as I could tell, most of the guys in my unit weren't Christians, and just about every night, you could find porn somewhere in the dorms. So, it was hard for me not to indulge. After all, I wanted to fit in. Even then, I refused to admit I had a problem. I told myself that I wasn't hurting anyone but myself. It wasn't until 2008, when

I arrived at my first duty station, that I acknowledged the problem to myself, and I attempted to quit.

I had tried quitting before, but I hadn't taken the crucial step of first admitting that I had a problem.

Because of that crucial missing step, I had some success, but I always turned back to the addiction for one reason or another, just like I had in the past. I knew something had to change, I wanted it to change, I wanted help, but I didn't know how to get it.

I couldn't admit my problem to anyone on base. What would they think of me? How would it affect my career? Could I lose my security clearance? I didn't know anyone in the churches we attended well enough to trust them. Plus, if I did say something, what would they think of me? I wouldn't be able to show my face in that church or community group again.

So, the co-dependent side of me took over, telling me that I could do it on my own, that I couldn't depend on anyone else to help me and keep my secret, not even my wife, so I kept it bottled up.

Rock Bottom and a New Beginning

Fast-forward to 2018. My church began its Celebrate Recovery ministry, and I remember thinking that I should check it out. But then the devil and my co-dependency would speak up and make me think twice about taking action.

I began thinking: Do I want to go to any church and admit that I look at porn, let alone doing so at the church where I'm actively attending and serving? What would they think? What would they think about my parents and how I was brought up? Would they ask me to leave the church? Would they permit me to continue serving and leading in the various ministries in which I was involved? I probably wouldn't be able to show my face there again.

It wasn't until December 2019 that I finally got the courage to attend my first meeting.

I remember pulling into the parking lot and feeling heavy. I considered just going home. But after deciding to go in, I said to myself, "I'll just sit in the back and not talk to anyone. Then I can say that I tried it, and it wasn't for me."

I can only picture Jesus sitting on His throne, laughing at me because He had other plans for me and my life. I went through the large group meeting and Newcomers 101, which is required for all new attendees. It's during 101 that they share more in-depth information about the program, how it works, and what you can expect each week.

During 101, I was asked what brought me in, and I said co-dependency, something I didn't even realize I struggled with until they explained it that night on stage, and a lightbulb went off in my head.

After I admitted to being co-dependent, the leader started to move on. Suddenly, he stopped, looked directly into my eyes, and asked, "Is there anything else?" At that moment, sirens began going off in my head.

What did he know? How did he know it? He had zero reason to ask that question. It isn't in the leader's script for 101 (I checked after the fact, and still find myself checking for it, as I now lead 101), and I began to weep. Before I could stop myself, I blurted out the secret I had carried for years and admitted my addiction to pornography.

I braced myself and waited for the reaction the devil had told me I would get. I was waiting for the leader to look shocked or disgusted with me and to tell me to leave. But instead, I got, "You are a brave man for admitting that. Thank you for your trust."

That moment shattered the shame I had carried for years. For the first time, I believed healing was possible. In that moment, the veil was lifted, and every lie the devil had told me was proven wrong.

Step 1 of Celebrate Recovery tells us that we must realize that we no longer have control over our addictions and habits, and that our lives are spiraling beyond our ability to manage them. Step 5 encourages us to be honest about our struggles—first with God, then with ourselves, and finally by opening up to someone we trust about the real issues we're facing.

In that moment of admitting my addiction to another human, a weight was lifted off my shoulders, a switch was flipped in my head, and my road to recovery began.

Today, I celebrate freedom from pornography, and for the first time, I care more about what God thinks than what people think.

The Prodigal Son and the Path to Freedom

Recently, I read a devotional for men, and one of the entries discussed the story of the prodigal son. You may know the story, but for those who don't, it revolves around a young man who didn't want to wait for his father to pass before receiving his inheritance. Instead, he wanted it immediately, and the father granted his son's request. The son went away from home and lived the lifestyle that he had dreamed about until, before he knew it, the money dried up.

Then, he found himself without money, food, or a home. He had hit rock bottom, which is what it took for him to see the error of his ways. He returned home and begged his father to allow him to live there once again. He even offered to work for his father and be a servant if that was what it took. But his father not only accepted him back, but he also threw a banquet in honor of his son's return.

It wasn't until I had a shift in the way I thought that I found freedom. Like the prodigal son, I had to realize that I couldn't survive on my own and that I needed the help of my heavenly Father. I had to return home and ask for His acceptance, forgiveness, and help!

Only then was I able to admit my struggles. Because of that, I now know that my value lies in what God thinks of me and my feelings about myself.

Each day, I continue to learn that it's okay not to be OK. It's okay to admit when I'm struggling, because my Rock is Jesus, and I know He's right there with me, encouraging me.

Death by a Different Name

I once heard a CR testimony in which the individual said that there were only two ways out of alcoholism: death or jail. I thought, "Man, I'm glad that my issues don't have death as a way out." But as time passed, his statement stayed with me, nagging me. I began to think about what he said differently, and as a result, I realized how wrong I had been. Sure, co-dependency and porn might not lead to physical death. But they do lead to death in many other areas.

Co-dependency kills your sense of self-worth and your ability to be the person God called you to be because it shifts your identity away from Christ and centers it on the approval of others. Instead of drawing your value from being a child of God, fearfully and wonderfully made, redeemed, and called with a purpose, you begin to base your worth on how others perceive you, treat you, or need you.

Over time, this can cause you, like it did me, to silence your voice, ignore your convictions, and suppress your God-given dreams—all for the sake of keeping the peace or meeting someone else's expectations. You become more reactive than proactive and anxious about rejection instead of being confident in your calling. Life becomes a prison of performance, where love feels conditional, and identity is always at risk of being lost.

Co-dependency trains you to ask, "What will they think?" instead of "What is right?" or "What does God think?" This clouds your discernment, hinders your spiritual growth, and makes walking in the freedom and authority God intends for you nearly impossible. Scripture says:

> *It is for freedom that Christ has set us free. Stand firm, then, and do not let yourselves be burdened again by a yoke of slavery.*
>
> —Galatians 5:1

Yet co-dependency shackles you to fear and people-pleasing, which are poor substitutes for the joy and peace found in God's approval.

The journey out of co-dependency starts with recognizing that your identity and value are *not* based on others' responses, but on who God says you are. Healing requires surrender, boundaries, and the courage to be honest with yourself, others, and God. Only then can you begin to build your self-worth on the unshakable foundation of God's truth and become the person He designed you to be.

Porn kills relationships. It might start secretly, hidden behind screens and rationalizations, but eventually it spills into every aspect of life. It rewires your brain to associate intimacy with isolation, self-gratification, and fantasy rather than love, connection, and commitment. Over time, it desensitizes your heart to the real needs of your spouse or future spouse and warps your expectations of love, affection, and physical intimacy.

It kills sexual drive, not by eliminating desire, but by redirecting it toward something counterfeit. Porn creates a dopamine-fueled cycle of highs and crashes, leaving you numb to the beauty and depth of true intimacy. What was meant to be a sacred, God-designed expression of unity between two people becomes cheapened, twisted, and addictive.

It changes the way you look at the opposite sex. Instead of seeing them as whole people, made in the image of God, you begin to see them through a lens of lust, consumption, and control. It turns individuals into objects, not souls.

You stop looking with compassion, honor, and respect. You start looking with entitlement or disinterest, unable to engage with others in a way that reflects God's love.

Perhaps most tragically, porn makes it difficult, though not impossible, to see others the way God intended you to. The damage is real, but so is the hope.

Healing begins with confession, accountability, and the gift of grace. God's vision for sex, love, and relationships is not shame-based or restrictive; it's redemptive, healing, and beautiful. Through Christ, minds can be renewed, eyes can be restored, and hearts can be transformed.

If you have struggled with pornography and had it distort your view like I did, God can give you new lenses to view the opposite sex through.

Do not conform to the pattern of this world, but be transformed by the renewing of your mind. Then you will be able to test and approve what God's will is—his good, pleasing and perfect will.

—Romans 12:2

Transformation is possible; I've experienced it, and trust me, it's worth fighting for. Today, I'm thankful for Celebrate Recovery and my journey to change my stars and free myself from the chains of addictions.

I'm grateful for a community of men who don't look down on me but see me for who I am and treat me as an equal. These are men who see my progress and call it out, who celebrate it with me. They are men who have chosen to lean on me for support and godly advice or wisdom, just as I provide for them in some cases.

I continue to work daily to be the best man I can be, the man that God has called me to be. This transformation journey didn't happen overnight. It's been a long road, and I'll continue to travel it for the rest of my life. But it's a road worth traveling, and I find comfort knowing I'm not alone.

Let's look now at some stories of transformation in the Bible that encourage me, and I pray will also encourage you in your journey to change your stars.

Section 2

Biblical Perspectives

Our stories don't exist in a vacuum. They're part of a much larger story that God has been writing since the beginning of time. In this section, we'll look at people in the Bible who experienced profound transformation.

They weren't perfect. They didn't always get it right. But they chose to trust God, and their lives were never the same. These stories aren't just history—they're roadmaps. And just like the stars they saw in their sky, these biblical lives can help guide us as we change our own.

Chapter 3
The Power of Transformation in the Bible

Biblical Stories of Transformation

The Bible is full of stories of transformation, such as Saul becoming Paul or the prodigal son finding his way back home. These stories remind us that no matter how far we have strayed, God will always forgive and welcome us back.

Saul Became Paul

Saul's conversion is one of Scripture's most powerful demonstrations of God's ability to redeem and repurpose a life. As a zealous Pharisee, Saul was not just indifferent to Christianity; he was violently opposed to it. He approved of the stoning of Stephen, the first Christian martyr, and made it his mission to arrest and persecute followers of Jesus. His reputation among early believers was one of fear and hostility.

But everything changed on the road to Damascus. A blinding light from heaven stopped him in his tracks, and he heard the voice of Jesus saying, *"Saul, Saul, why do you persecute me"* (Acts 9:4)?

In that divine encounter, Saul came face-to-face with the risen Christ. He was struck blind for three days, during which his physical sight was taken, but his spiritual vision was just beginning to awaken.

Through the obedience of a believer named Ananias, Saul's sight was restored, and he was filled with the Holy Spirit. From that moment forward, Saul began a radical new journey, not as a persecutor of the faith, but as its boldest proclaimer. He became Paul, the apostle to the Gentiles, a church planter, mentor, and author of much of the New Testament.

Paul's story is proof that no one is beyond the reach of God's grace. His life is a testament to the fact that transformation is possible when we encounter Jesus, no matter how far we've fallen or how frightening our past.

Prodigal Son

Then there is the story of the prodigal son, which I referenced earlier. The younger son, unwilling to wait for his father to die to receive his inheritance, decided instead to demand it from his father right then and there. The father, most likely against his better judgment, agreed and gave it to him.

The son dove headfirst into a life of partying and reckless pleasure, wasting it all on reckless living until one day, his inheritance was gone. Then he could no longer live as he had been.

This became his reality check. When he finally came to his senses, he returned home to his father, expecting to be rejected, and offering to work for his father as a servant. But instead, his father welcomed him with open arms, telling the servants to fetch new clothes for his son and throwing a party to celebrate his return.

This is a story of transformation and of a love that mirrors God's heart. The prodigal son was transformed from a selfish and ungrateful son to a humble and grateful one, while the father demonstrated a Christ-like love for his son.

Like the prodigal son, I took my inheritance from God for granted. I spent years trying to live for myself, lost in addiction, while still trying to appear as if I was living for Him.

But it wasn't until I humbled myself, returned to my Father, and asked for His forgiveness that everything changed. A banquet was thrown in Heaven, and I began to walk again in a newfound freedom.

The Story of Moses

Moses is often an overlooked story of transformation. He was a Hebrew baby born during a time when the Pharaoh had ordered that all Hebrew baby boys be killed. Moses's mother hid him for three months, but when she could no longer conceal him, she placed him in a basket and set it afloat in the Nile River. The Pharaoh's daughter found Moses and adopted him as her son.

Moses grew up in the Egyptian palace but was always aware of his Hebrew heritage. One day, when he was an adult, he saw an Egyptian beating a Hebrew slave, so he killed the Egyptian and fled Egypt.

He lived in the desert for forty years. During that time, he married and had a son. While Moses was tending his flock one day, he saw a burning bush. The voice of God spoke to Moses from the bush and told him to return to Egypt and lead the Hebrews out of slavery.

Moses was reluctant at first, but eventually agreed to go. He returned to Egypt and confronted Pharaoh, demanding that he let the Hebrews go. Pharaoh refused, and God sent a series of plagues to punish Egypt. Finally, after the tenth plague, Pharaoh agreed to let the Hebrews go.

Moses led the Hebrews out of Egypt and into the desert, where they wandered for forty years until they reached the Promised Land. Moses died before the Hebrews entered the Promised Land, but he is considered one of the most influential figures in the Bible.

Moses's transformation didn't begin in the palace; it began in the wilderness when God met him in a burning bush. He realized that God was calling him to do something meaningful. He was reluctant at first, but he eventually agreed to go. This was the beginning of his transformation from a shepherd to a leader.

His transformation was not easy. He faced many challenges, including the Pharaoh, the plagues, and wandering in the desert. But through it all, he remained faithful to God. He led the Hebrews to freedom and to the edge of the Promised Land. Moses's transformation serves as a reminder that God can use anyone, regardless of their background or circumstances. He can transform us into leaders who can make a difference in the world.

These stories remind us that God is always willing to forgive us and transform our lives. No matter how far we have strayed, we can always come back to Him.

Key Teachings on Change, Growth, and Renewal

The Bible teaches that change, growth, and renewal are all possible through God's power when we come to Him and ask. In the Old Testament, the prophet Jeremiah spoke of God's promise to renew His people:

> *I will give you a new heart and put a new spirit in you; I will remove from you your heart of stone and give you a heart of flesh.*
>
> —Ezekiel 36:26

This promise is fulfilled in the New Testament when Jesus offers us new life through His death and resurrection. When we repent, turn away from sin and toward God, and believe in Jesus, we are born again.

Jesus replied, "Very truly I tell you, no one can see the kingdom of God unless they are born again."

"How can someone be born when they are old?" Nicodemus asked. "Surely they cannot enter a second time into their mother's womb to be born!"

Jesus answered, "Very truly I tell you, no one can enter the kingdom of God unless they are born of water and the Spirit."

—John 3:3–5

This new birth gives us a new heart and spirit, enabling us to live a life of change, growth, and renewal. The Bible teaches that change is a process that takes time and effort.

Therefore, we do not lose heart. Though outwardly we are wasting away, yet inwardly we are being renewed day by day. For our light and momentary troubles are achieving for us an eternal glory that far outweighs them all. So, we fix our eyes not on what is seen, but on what is unseen, since what is seen is temporary, but what is unseen is eternal.

—2 Corinthians 4:16–18

We are not perfect, and we will continue to make mistakes. The most profound changes often happen on the inside, long before they're visible on the outside.

God is patient with us and helps us grow and change over time. The Bible also teaches that growth is a journey, not a destination. We'll never reach perfection, but we can move steadily toward purpose as we walk with God. Romans 3:23 says, *"for all have sinned and fall short of the glory of God."*

I am certainly not perfect and will not pretend to be. However, we are to live in this world but not be of this world. Scripture says, *"For though we live in the world, we do not wage war as the world does"* (2 Corinthians 10:3).

Finally, the Bible teaches that renewal is a gift from God. We cannot renew ourselves on our own, but God can give us a new heart and a new spirit. When we repent and believe in Jesus, we are forgiven and made new. We are given a fresh start and can live a life of change, growth, and renewal.

I encourage you to turn to God if you want change, growth, and renewal. He is the only one who can truly change you from the inside out.

The stories and teachings found within the Bible offer a wellspring of inspiration that can ignite the spark of transformation within us. These narratives, filled with relatable characters and profound lessons, provide a roadmap for personal growth and change.

How These Stories Inspire Us Today

Here are some insights into how these stories and teachings can inspire us to embark on our transformational journey:

Identification with Characters

The Bible is full of characters who faced challenges, doubts, and setbacks like those you've already read about here. We can identify with their struggles and recognize that even those deemed as having remarkable faith experienced moments of uncertainty. Identifying with them can help us overcome our doubts and fears, knowing that transformation is possible even amid trials.

Hope Amidst Adversity

Stories of triumph over adversity, like the tale of Joseph's rise from slavery to leadership, infuse us with hope. These narratives remind us that challenges are not insurmountable obstacles but growth opportunities. We can find inspiration in the resilience of these characters and envision their transformative potential.

Redemption and Second Chances

The theme of redemption resonates throughout the Bible, illustrating that mistakes do not define us indefinitely. The story of the prodigal son's return and forgiveness highlights the power of second chances. Those grappling with regret can find solace and motivation to embrace change, knowing that they, too, can experience renewal.

Vision of Divine Purpose

Many biblical figures, such as Moses, discovered their unique purposes and roles in pivotal moments. These stories emphasize that each of us is a part of God's grand narrative and design. We can be inspired to search for our purpose and use it as a driving force for transformation.

Lessons from Mistakes

The Bible's candid portrayal of humanity's flaws provides valuable lessons. For instance, the story of Peter's denial and subsequent reconciliation with Jesus teaches the importance of humility, forgiveness, and self-awareness. Acknowledging and rectifying our shortcomings can help us learn from these mistakes and seek personal growth.

Faith as a Catalyst

Stories of faith, such as the account of the woman who touched Jesus's garment to be healed, illustrate the transformative power of unwavering belief. We can draw inspiration from these accounts, realizing that our faith can be a catalyst for change, enabling us to overcome obstacles and move toward our own desired transformation.

Transformative Teachings

Beyond stories, the Bible contains teachings that encourage inner change. The Sermon on the Mount's teachings on humility, compassion, and forgiveness inspire us to cultivate virtues that contribute to personal transformation. These teachings provide a roadmap for not only changing actions but also transforming the core of one's being.

Shared Humanity

The Bible's universal themes of love, compassion, and unity remind us of our shared humanity. These themes should inspire us to connect with others on a deeper level and extend empathy, fostering an environment conducive to mutual growth and transformation. As we reflect on these lessons, it's clear that Scripture isn't just a record of what God *did* but a living invitation to what He still *does*.

When we see our struggles reflected in Scripture, it reminds us that we're not alone. These stories, and the God behind them, call us to embrace change, pursue growth, and realign our lives with divine purpose. That's how we begin to change our "stars."

Chapter 4
Understanding Your Current Stars – The Stars That Shape Our Lives

The metaphor of "stars" as symbols of the different facets of our lives is both poetic and profound, offering a unique lens through which we can view life's journey. Just as stars dot the night sky, many aspects of our lives impact our direction. Relationships, careers, health, and spirituality act as guiding stars—illuminating the ever-changing tapestry of our lives.

Reflecting on the Stars of Our Lives

Reflecting on the "star" concept brings several insights to light. The first insight is that of diverse constellations. Just as constellations vary in arrangement and brightness, so do the constellations of our lives. Each person's constellation is a unique arrangement of stars, representing their experiences, challenges, and achievements. Just as the cosmos captivates us with its diversity, our lives are enriched by the array of experiences we encounter in each facet.

Like Moses's journey, from palace to wilderness to purpose, our life constellations may initially seem chaotic. But over time, God reveals how each star, even the dim ones, is part of a greater design.

Second, there are the guiding stars. Stars have guided travelers for millennia, providing direction and assurance. Similarly, our relationships, careers, health, and spirituality are guiding stars, pointing us toward purpose and fulfillment.

Just like sailors once relied on stars for direction, we look to our most prominent life areas to guide our decisions and values. For some, that means navigating based on their career; for some, it's family; and for others, faith serves as the guiding star from which they get direction.

The third guiding reflection to consider is that of balance and harmony. Constellations maintain a delicate equilibrium in the night sky, with each star playing a role in the overall composition. Similarly, the harmony among our relationships, careers, health, and spirituality contributes to our well-being. Striving for balance in these areas ensures that our life's constellation remains vibrant and coherent.

The prodigal son lost all balance when he chased temporary pleasures, but his return home shows how quickly God can restore harmony when we realign with Him.

Even when we find balance, our constellations are still in flux. The night sky is ever-changing, with stars rising and setting, much like the ebb and flow of our lives. Recognizing the impermanence of circumstances reminds us to cherish moments of brightness and to navigate through challenges with resilience, knowing that they're temporary and that new stars will emerge.

This reminds us that nothing in our lives exists in isolation. Just as stars are part of a vast cosmic web, our different life aspects are also interconnected. Strong faith can enhance our relationships, while good health can positively influence our career aspirations. Acknowledging these interdependencies allows us to make intentional choices that enrich multiple areas simultaneously.

One could argue, however, that we shape our own destiny. The metaphor of stars symbolizes our role as architects of our constellations. We have the power to arrange the importance of our relationships, careers, health, and faith to form a narrative that aligns with our deepest aspirations.

Just as ancient astronomers charted the heavens, we can chart the course of our lives, and unlike astronomers, we can alter the course of our lives through our life choices.

But as with anything, there are mysteries and exploration to be had. The night sky has long held a sense of wonder and mystery, inviting us to explore its depths. Similarly, our journey through relationships, careers, health, and spirituality is a voyage of discovery. Embracing the unknown with curiosity allows us to uncover new insights and possibilities.

All this will leave a legacy that radiates in the lives of those we love long after we are gone. When stars shine brightly, their light travels through time, leaving a legacy that endures. Likewise, the impact we create in our relationships, careers, health, and spirituality can reverberate beyond our immediate circumstances, impacting the lives of others and leaving a lasting imprint.

In contemplating the concept of "stars" representing the multifaceted dimensions of our lives, we recognize that just as stars contribute to the beauty and vastness of the cosmos, our relationships, careers, health, and spirituality contribute to the richness and depth of our lives. When we live with intention and balance, the light from our "stars" begins to reflect who we truly are and the story God is writing.

Tools for Assessing Your Life's Constellation

Now that we've explored how "stars" shape our lives, let's examine a few tools that can help us assess where we are and where we want to go.

Strengths and Weaknesses Analysis

This exercise can help you identify your strengths and weaknesses in various aspects of your life, providing insight into areas where transformation is possible.

How to do it:

- List a life area (e.g., relationships, career, or health) at the top of a sheet of paper.
- Now divide that page into two columns: strengths and weaknesses.
- Reflect on your life and list your strengths and weaknesses in the appropriate columns.

Doing this exercise will help you to reflect on leveraging your strengths to improve weak areas and address weaknesses.

Goal Setting

Goal setting provides a structured approach to creating transformation by setting specific objectives in each life area.

How to do it:

- Select a life area you want to transform.
- Set a specific goal that is measurable, achievable, relevant, and time-bound (SMART).

- Break down the goal into actionable steps.
- Track your progress and adjust as needed.

SWOT Analysis

Adapting the business-oriented SWOT analysis helps you identify strengths, weaknesses, opportunities, and threats in each life aspect.

How to do it:

- Create a table with four columns: Strengths, Weaknesses, Opportunities, and Threats.
- Fill in each column with relevant points for a specific life area.
- Analyze the results to identify areas where transformation is needed.

For example, let's look at a SWOT analysis of a relationship.

Strengths:
- List positive aspects of the relationship such as mutual respect, effective communication, shared values, etc.

Weaknesses:
- Identify areas of improvement or challenges within the relationship, such as communication issues, lack of quality time together, differences in future goals, etc.

Opportunities:
- Consider opportunities for growth and improvement in the relationship, such as attending couples counseling,

trying new activities together, setting relationship goals, etc.

Threats:
- Identify external or internal factors that could potentially harm the relationship, such as external stressors like financial difficulties, work-related issues, family conflicts, or internal challenges like trust issues, unresolved conflicts, etc.

You can organize this information into a four-quadrant table with each quadrant representing one aspect of the SWOT analysis. Use different colors or styles to differentiate between strengths, weaknesses, opportunities, and threats. Be sure to keep the design clear and easy to read.

Time Audit

A time audit helps you understand how you allocate your time and whether that aligns with your priorities for transformation.

How to do it:
- Track your activities and how much time you spend on them for a week.
- Categorize the activities into different life areas (relationships, career, health, etc.).
- Reflect on whether your time allocation aligns with your transformation goals.

Vision Board

Creating a vision board visually represents your desired transformation in each life area, keeping your goals in focus.

How to do it:

- Collect images, quotes, and words that represent your aspirations for each life area.
- Create a physical or digital collage with these elements.
- Display your vision board where you can see it regularly for motivation and focus.

Of all these tools, the next two have been especially powerful in my own journey, and I recommend them for those who are trying to make healthy adjustments in their lives to see a change in their stars.

Going Deeper with Journaling

Use journaling prompts to encourage self-reflection and exploration of your feelings, aspirations, and challenges in various aspects of your life.

How to do it:

- Select a life aspect you would like to evaluate.
- Write freely about your thoughts, feelings, and experiences related to that aspect.
- Use prompts like these: What do I want to change? What challenges do I face? How do I envision transformation in this area?

I've provided a couple of questions for each area of your life that you can use to get yourself started. This is especially useful if you're new to journaling. The important thing here is to be honest with yourself and not filter your responses. Just write what comes to mind.

Relationships:

- Reflect on your closest relationships. What dynamics bring you joy, and which ones might need improvement?
- Describe a recent interaction that left you feeling positive. What can you learn from this interaction to enhance other relationships?
- Are there any unresolved conflicts or misunderstandings in your relationships? How might you approach resolving them?

Career:

- What aspects of your current career or job bring you fulfillment and satisfaction?
- Do you have skills or talents that you're not utilizing in your current role? How might you incorporate them more effectively?
- Envision your ideal workday. What tasks, responsibilities, and environment contribute to your sense of purpose and happiness?

Health and Well-Being:

- How do you feel physically, mentally, and emotionally daily? Are there any areas that need more attention?

- Reflect on your eating habits and exercise routine. Are they aligned with your health goals? If not, how can you make positive changes?

Spirituality:

- How do you currently connect with your faith and sense of purpose?
- What practices are you doing that bring you peace and a stronger connection with God?
- Are there any areas of your faith that you've been curious about exploring more? How do you see them contributing to your personal growth?

Personal Growth:

- Reflect on a recent challenge or setback you faced. How did you respond, and what did you learn from the experience?
- Consider your strengths and weaknesses. How can you leverage your strengths to address areas in need of improvement?
- What areas of personal growth have you been postponing? How can you take steps to actively pursue them?

Hobbies and Passions:

- List the activities or hobbies that bring you joy and fulfillment. How often do you engage in them?
- What interests or passions have you set aside due to lack of time or other commitments? How might you reintegrate them into your life?

Time Management:

- Reflect on how you spend your time each day. Are there activities that consume a significant portion of your day without contributing to your growth or well-being?
- Identify one time-consuming habit you'd like to change. How can you reclaim that time for more meaningful pursuits?

Mindfulness and Gratitude:

- Take a moment to reflect on your thoughts and emotions. What recurring patterns or concerns do you notice?
- List three things you're grateful for today. How can you incorporate gratitude into your daily routine to enhance your perspective?

Self-Care and Relaxation:

- Reflect on how you recharge and practice self-care. Are there areas in which you neglect your well-being?
- Imagine a perfect day of relaxation and self-care. What activities would you engage in, and how can you incorporate them regularly?

Social Connections:

- Consider the quality of your social interactions and connections. Do you feel supported and valued by your social circle?
- Reflect on a recent meaningful conversation. How did it impact you, and how can you foster more of these connections?

The Power of Mentorship and Real Friendship

Mentor or Coach Interaction

This method is my favorite for both self-reflection and growth. Many biblical passages tell us to support one another and to carry each other's burdens. We are not meant to travel the roads of life alone. Guidance from counselors, mentors, coaches, or trusted friends offers external perspectives on our circumstances and areas that need transformation.

The key here is finding one or two people (preferably of the same sex) with whom you can do life and be 100 percent real. If you're married, find another couple with whom you can be honest and real. Because if you're not honest with them, then the advice they give you won't be as helpful as you need.

This is especially true if you're seeing a counselor or therapist. I've found that people think that counselors or therapists can only be of help if they're struggling with mental health issues. When in fact, that's not true; they can help with so much more. They can be a sounding board to help you work through things and can even provide you with additional exercises or resources to help target a specific area of your life that you feel needs to be adjusted.

How to do it:

- Identify individuals you trust and respect for their insights.
- Discuss your goals, challenges, and aspirations with them.
- Listen to their feedback and suggestions for areas that could benefit from transformation.

Just as Paul needed Barnabas to walk alongside him after his dramatic transformation, we, too, need people who see our potential, even when we're still figuring it out.

My Experience and Encouragement to You

I have gone through the journey of learning to understand my current stars, and it can be tough. But let me tell you, it is so worth it. By following some of the techniques described in this chapter, you can get a good understanding of where you are and how you got there. From there, you can begin to understand what changes need to be made to alter your course and change your stars.

The tools and exercises I found most useful were journaling, counseling, and having a mentor (or two) to examine my life with and provide guidance.

Full disclosure: Journaling was—and still is—very hard for me. I hate writing about my feelings, and I often find myself wanting to filter my words as I write. It's taken a lot of practice to allow myself to feel the emotions of life and find the words to write (or type) in my journal.

But by forcing myself to sit and write, I've been able to dig into things deeper than I ever had and express myself to others through letter writing. Some of those letters will never see the light of day, but by writing them, I've been able to process feelings and move past things that were bothering me at the time.

Likewise, I have found much freedom using counselors and good friends. When I first started going to a professional counselor and talking with other Christian men, I did it to check a box. I didn't open up to them because I felt that "I didn't need it." I was only there to make others happy. If that's you, let me encourage you to give counseling and mentoring a shot. Open up; be raw and honest with them and with yourself.

There is **nothing** like a friendship that's genuinely an iron-sharpens-iron relationship. What I have in mind is a relationship in which you can both be completely honest with each other about what you're going through in life without the fear of being judged or rejected. In such a genuine relationship, you can speak life and truth into each other and support each other when times are hard.

I can only say that I've had such relationships a couple of times in my life, and they are the ones that I value above all others. These people are friends—no, better yet, they are brothers for life, and I know that whenever I need them, they are there for me as I am for them.

I can discuss relationships, my career, and whatever else comes to mind with them, and I know they will listen and offer sound advice when I ask for it. Likewise, my counselor has been an invaluable resource for examining my personal life, identifying areas that require improvement, and giving me tools to make those improvements.

Closing Reflection

As you consider the stars that shape your current constellation, what needs to be realigned? What guiding light are you following, and where is it taking you?

Remember that *"he determines the number of the stars and calls them each by name" (Psalm 147:4)*. And that includes you.

Before we close this chapter, take a few minutes to pause, pray, and ask God what He wants to show you through your current constellation.

A Prayer for Realignment

Father,

Thank You for being the One who not only hung the stars but knows each one by name, including mine.

As I look at my life, help me to see clearly the things I've made central that were never meant to guide me. Show me where I've followed false lights, comfort, fear, performance, approval, and gently lead me back to You.

Give me wisdom to examine my life with honesty, grace to face what needs to change, and courage to make those changes. Help me to realign my relationships, my purpose, my habits, and my heart to reflect Your will.

Teach me to walk in Your light, so that the constellation of my life points others to You.

In Jesus's name,

Amen.

Journaling Challenge: Charting Your Constellation

Use the following questions to reflect honestly on your life. Write without filtering or judging—observe and listen.

1. What are the "brightest stars" guiding me right now?
   (Think: career, family, achievement, faith, etc.)

2. Are there stars I've been following that no longer align with who I want to become?

3. Which biblical figure's transformation most reflects the season I'm in right now? Why?

4. If God were to rearrange one part of my life constellation, what would I hope He would touch first?

5. What is one star I want to give more attention to in this season—and what's one small step I can take toward that?

Chapter 5
The Divine Blueprint: God's Design for Your Life

It doesn't matter who you talk to, or what their faith beliefs are, there is a good chance that they believe in a higher power of some kind. I believe that every individual possesses a unique purpose crafted by God. This foundational and deeply spiritual concept has profoundly shaped the philosophies and worldviews of countless people throughout history.

At the core of this idea lies the notion that there is a divine plan for each person, intricately woven into the fabric of the universe. Each life is a constellation in God's sky—carefully placed, perfectly timed, and shining for a purpose greater than we can often see. This plan is like a grand tapestry, with everyone's life forming an essential thread. Just as no two snowflakes are identical, no two destinies are alike, and this uniqueness is to be celebrated.

This belief instills a sense of great significance and purpose in each person's life. It helps us believe that our existence is not random, but purposeful. It helps us feel like we are part of a grand design, carefully orchestrated by a higher intelligence. This design encompasses not only our external circumstances but also our inner qualities, talents, and passions.

For those who hold this belief, life becomes a quest to discover and fulfill their divine purpose. It's a journey marked by introspection, faith, and alignment with their inner calling. Many people find that as they delve deeper into understanding their purpose, they experience a profound sense of connection to God and the world, along with a greater sense of meaning in their existence.

However, it's important to note that belief in a unique purpose doesn't mean that you have a life free of challenges and hardships. Life's challenges and hardships are an integral part of our human experience. With each one comes unique opportunities for growth and learning. Additionally, they give us a chance to look at and refine our character.

The feeling of having a divine purpose and being an integral part of a grander picture can also bring a sense of responsibility. If each person's destiny is part of a larger divine plan, their choices and actions carry weight and significance.

Ultimately, the belief in a unique purpose and destiny designed by God is a powerful source of inspiration and motivation for many individuals. Our relationship with God and the Bible provides a framework through which we can make sense of our lives, find meaning in our experiences, and strive for a sense of fulfillment that transcends the mundane aspects of existence.

Aligning with God's plan is a transformative journey rooted in the belief that true fulfillment arises from surrendering to divine guidance. This concept, deeply ingrained in various religious traditions, is expressed in biblical passages that highlight God's active role in shaping the lives of individuals. Jeremiah 29:11 says:

For I know the plans I have for you," declares the Lord, "plans to prosper you and not to harm you, plans to give you hope and a future."

This assurance suggests that God's plans are purposeful, leading to a future filled with hope and well-being. The alignment with God's plan is not a passive acceptance but an active seeking, as expressed in Proverbs 3:5–6:

Trust in the Lord with all your heart and lean not on your own understanding; in all your ways submit to him, and he will make your paths straight.

This submission is an intentional act, a testament to trust in divine wisdom that transcends human comprehension.

True fulfillment emerges from recognizing God's sovereignty and seeking alignment with His purpose. This is further affirmed in Psalm 37:23, which says: "*The Lord makes firm the steps of the one who delights in him.*"

This delight implies aligning desires with God's will, paving the way for a life journey guided by divine principles. Ephesians 2:10 further reinforces this idea, saying:

For we are God's handiwork, created in Christ Jesus to do good works, which God prepared in advance for us to do.

Here, the notion of being God's handiwork signifies a deliberate and purposeful creation, everyone uniquely designed for a specific role in fulfilling divine plans. The transformative nature of aligning with God's plan is emphasized in Romans 12:2, which says to believers:

Do not conform to the pattern of this world, but be transformed by the renewing of your mind. Then you will be able to test and approve what God's will is—his good, pleasing and perfect will.

This transformation involves a renewal of the mind, a shift in perspective that allows individuals to discern and align with God's perfect will. The journey of alignment is dynamic, involving continual growth and refinement, as expressed in Proverbs 16:9:

In their hearts humans plan their course, but the Lord establishes their steps.

Here, human planning coexists with divine intervention, illustrating the ongoing collaboration between human agency and God's guiding influence. In essence, aligning with God's plan leads to true fulfillment by acknowledging His wisdom, actively seeking alignment, and finding purpose in the intentional design of an individual's life. This alignment is not a guarantee of a trouble-free existence, but a promise of resilience and hope amid life's challenges.

The transformative power of this alignment is a continual process of renewal, a journey toward becoming the individual God intended, as expressed in Psalm 139:16:

Your eyes saw my unformed body; all the days ordained for me were written in your book before one of them came to be.

This recognition of a preordained plan underscores the profound nature of the journey toward true fulfillment and transformation through alignment with God's purpose.

Let's take a deeper dive into the stories of biblical figures who faced challenges and embraced transformation, such as Abraham, Joseph, and Esther. Together we can learn from their faith and experiences to help us navigate our own journeys of change.

Abraham's Story

Abraham, often referred to as the "Father of Faith," is a pivotal figure in the Bible. His story in the book of Genesis provides profound insights into facing challenges and embracing transformation. His journey, marked by faith, trials, and transformation, holds timeless lessons for those navigating their paths of change.

Though Abraham had no map, he followed the stars of God's promises into the unknown, trusting that each step was divinely charted. God's promises were the stars by which he charted his course; though distant and mysterious, they pulled him forward.

Abraham's narrative begins with a divine call in Genesis 12, where God instructs him to leave his country, his people, and his father's household to go to a land that God will show him. Here, the first lesson unfolds.

1. ***Embrace the Unknown with Faith.*** Abraham demonstrated remarkable faith by responding to God's call and entering an uncertain future. He chose to leave everything he knew and loved behind to follow what he believed was God's call on his life. This echoes a universal truth: Meaningful transformation often requires stepping into the unknown with trust and confidence.

   As Abraham journeys, he encounters various trials, including a famine that leads him to Egypt and later conflicts over land. These challenges embody the second lesson.

2. ***Trials are Opportunities for Growth.*** Abraham's story teaches us that challenges are not always obstacles and can serve as catalysts for personal and spiritual growth. For Abraham, each trial becomes a refining process, shaping him into the person he was destined to become.

   The apex of Abraham's journey comes in Genesis 22 when God commands him to sacrifice his beloved son, Isaac. That narrative reveals the third lesson.

3. ***God's Timing Is Perfect.*** The birth of Isaac in their old age (Abraham was 100 years old, and Sarah was 90) emphasizes that God's promises are fulfilled in His timing, which may not align with human expectations.

   I don't know about you, but I can't imagine having a newborn baby at 100 or 90 years old. But this story teaches us the importance of patience and of trusting God's divine timeline in our journey through life.

4. ***Surrender and Obedience Bring Transformation.*** Abraham's willingness to surrender his most cherished possession (Genesis 22) demonstrates profound obedience to God. In this act of surrender, Abraham undergoes a transformative encounter with the divine, and God provides a ram as a substitute for the sacrifice. The story highlights the transformative power of surrendering our most cherished aspects, allowing God to work in unexpected ways.

   As if this wasn't enough, Abraham's earlier life was further characterized by patience, waiting to fulfill God's promise of a son. Despite his age and Sarah's barrenness, Abraham learned the fourth lesson.

These lessons from Abraham's life provide a roadmap for those navigating their journeys of change.

Joseph's Story

Now, let's examine Joseph's story, which is also found in the book of Genesis. It is a compelling saga of resilience, forgiveness, and transformative change.

Joseph's life is marked by a series of challenges that lead to his rise from slavery and imprisonment to becoming a prominent figure in Egypt. His story holds valuable lessons for us as we navigate our own journeys of change.

Joseph's journey begins with betrayal at perhaps the deepest level. His brothers, the people who were supposed to be in his corner and cheering him on throughout his life, betrayed him by selling him into slavery out of jealousy. It's this initial challenge that sets the stage for the first lesson.

1. **Resilience in the Face of Betrayal.** Despite adversity, Joseph remains steadfast, demonstrating resilience in the face of personal betrayal. This resilience becomes a crucial factor in his eventual rise to prominence.

   In Potiphar's house, Joseph faces another challenge when he is unjustly accused of raping Potiphar's wife and is thrown into prison. This is where the second lesson emerges.

2. **Adversity as a Stepping Stone.** Joseph's time in prison becomes a transformative period. He utilizes his God-given gift of interpreting dreams to gain favor and ultimately secure his release.

This teaches us that, though challenges may initially seem daunting, they can be stepping stones toward transformation and growth. They may be just the tool we need to begin realigning our stars.

Joseph's ability to interpret dreams leads to an audience with Pharaoh and his appointment as a high-ranking official. This progression illustrates the third lesson.

3. **God's Hand in Divine Appointments.** Joseph recognizes that his ascent is not a result of his efforts, but a divine appointment orchestrated by God. This lesson should encourage us to look for and acknowledge the holy hand of God in our own life events.

This next part of Joseph's story is one of my favorites. You see, the pinnacle of Joseph's story is revealed when he confronts his brothers, who had betrayed him. Instead of seeking revenge, which I'd wager to say any one of us would do, Joseph chooses to forgive them, exemplifying the fourth lesson.

4. **The Transformative Power of Forgiveness**. Joseph's act of forgiveness becomes a catalyst for reconciliation and familial restoration. This lesson highlights the transformative power of genuine forgiveness in personal relationships.

Drawing from my own experiences, I can relate to Joseph's journey in facing unexpected challenges and the need for resilience. In times of personal betrayal or loss, I found strength in the knowledge that these events are stepping stones, though hard, toward personal growth. Just as Joseph's time in prison was transformative, my periods of difficulty became opportunities for self-reflection and learning.

Moreover, Joseph's recognition of divine appointments resonates with my own understanding that certain life events were beyond my control and that trusting in a higher power (God) and His plan provides solace and guidance.

Finally, Joseph's act of forgiveness aligns with my journey in recognizing the transformative power of letting go of resentment and embracing forgiveness because you can't begin moving on and changing your stars until you complete this step.

In essence, Joseph's story offers a roadmap for navigating journeys of change. His story illustrates that challenges, though formidable, can be catalysts for transformative change. By embodying resilience, viewing adversity as an opportunity, acknowledging divine appointments, and embracing forgiveness, we can navigate our journeys of change with purpose and transformation.

Joseph's life wasn't a random series of events; it was a constellation of divine moments, each leading him to fulfill his purpose.

Story of Esther

Finally, let's look at one more story. This time, it is Esther's story, a captivating narrative of courage, purpose, and transformation.

Esther, a Jewish orphan raised by her cousin Mordecai, becomes the Queen of Persia at a critical juncture. Her story, as recorded in the book of Esther, offers valuable lessons for us as we navigate our journeys of change.

Esther's journey begins when she is chosen as a candidate for the king's harem. Her initial challenge is to keep her identity as a Jew hidden. This circumstance sets the stage for the first lesson.

1. **Embracing Identity in the Face of Adversity.** Esther's eventual disclosure of her identity illustrates the power of authenticity, even in the face of potential risks.

   Esther's star rose at just the right time, *"for such a time as this"* (Esther 4:14), proving that God's alignment is always intentional. Her courage and calling were already part of God's design, just waiting for the right moment to shine.

   Today, it can be very easy for us to become co-dependent, caring more about what others think of us than what we think of ourselves or, even better, what God thinks of us. This gives us an overwhelming desire to hide our true selves just so we can "fit in" with those around us.

   I discussed my journey with co-dependency earlier, referring to myself as a "master chameleon." Over time, I got so good at blending in that I lost sight of who I was.

   Being able to blend into just about any environment is a great skill to have, but not at the price of losing your own identity. Over the years, through considerable effort, I've begun to find myself again, and I'm discovering that embracing and being true to myself is a source of strength amid challenges.

   The central crisis in Esther's story arises when Haman, a high-ranking official, plots to annihilate all the Jewish people in Persia. Mordecai urges Esther to intercede, leading to the second lesson.

2. **Courageous Action in the Face of Injustice.** Esther faces the risk of approaching the king uninvited, which was punishable by death. Her willingness to take this bold step reflects the transformative power of courage in the pursuit of justice.

In my personal life, I've learned that taking courageous actions, even when they seem daunting, is often a catalyst for personal growth. Esther's plea to the king results in saving her people, showcasing the third lesson.

3. **Embracing One's Unique Calling.** Though initially reluctant, Esther steps into her role as a leader with a sense of purpose. This lesson highlights the significance of recognizing and embracing one's unique calling, which can lead to profound transformation. The conclusion of Esther's story emphasizes the fourth lesson.

4. **Celebrating and Remembering Transformative Moments.** The Jewish festival of Purim commemorates the Jewish people's deliverance. This lesson encourages us to honor and remember transformative moments in our own lives. Reflecting on and commemorating moments of growth and change can be a source of inspiration for the ongoing journey.

Esther's story serves as a beacon of inspiration, urging us to face challenges authentically, take courageous actions, embrace our unique callings, and celebrate transformative moments. These lessons, drawn from Esther's experiences, guide us as we navigate our journeys of change.

These three stories have a lot of wisdom packed into them. In fact, this chapter is only just beginning to scratch the surface of the lessons we can learn from the lives of Abraham, Joseph, and Esther and the experiences they went through.

Let's pause for a moment and examine the principles derived from the stories of Abraham, Joseph, and Esther. Like stars in the night sky, they shine to guide us on our path to transformation:

- **Embrace the Unknown with Faith:** Trust in divine guidance and step into the future with faith.

- **View Trials as Opportunities for Growth**: See challenges as stepping stones for personal and spiritual development.

- **Surrender and Obedience Bring Transformation:** Be willing to surrender to a higher purpose, obeying divine plans.

- **God's Timing Is Perfect:** Patiently await the fulfillment of promises, recognizing the divine timing.

- **Cultivate Resilience in the Face of Betrayal:** Maintain steadfastness and resilience in the face of personal betrayals.

- **Recognize God's Hand in Divine Appointments:** Acknowledge the divine orchestrations in life events, trusting in a higher plan.

- **Embrace the Transformative Power of Forgiveness**: Choose forgiveness as a catalyst for personal and relational restoration.

- **Embrace Identity Authentically:** Be authentic in embracing and expressing your identity, even in adversity.

- **Take Courageous Action in Pursuit of Justice:** Act boldly and courageously, especially when faced with injustice and risks.

- **Recognize and Embrace Your Unique Calling:** Acknowledge and embrace the unique calling and purpose in life.

- **Celebrate and Remember Transformative Moments**: Reflect on and commemorate moments of growth and change for ongoing inspiration.

Together, these truths form a constellation of wisdom—a divine blueprint—meant to guide us through the darkest nights and the brightest days.

A Prayer for Alignment and Courage

Father,

Thank You for crafting a unique purpose for my life and calling me into a divine plan bigger than I could ever imagine. Even when I don't understand the path, help me trust in You, the One who charts the stars and directs every step.

Please give me Abraham's faith to walk boldly into the unknown, Joseph's resilience to endure trials with hope, and Esther's courage to stand firm in my calling.

Align my heart and desires with Yours. Make my heart sensitive to Your voice and cause my will to surrender to Your purpose. Help me remember that every detour, delay, and difficulty has a place in the tapestry you're weaving.

Use me, Lord, to reflect Your glory like stars in the sky, and may the legacy of my life point others back to You. And may every step I take in obedience become a star in the sky of Your story.

In Jesus's name,

Amen.

Journaling Challenge: Discovering Your Blueprint

Reflect on and respond to these journaling prompts to deepen the chapter's impact on your life:

1. What moments in my life have felt "divinely appointed"? How might God have used them for growth or redirection?

2. Which of the stories—Abraham, Joseph, or Esther—do I most relate to right now? Why?

3. What part of God's purpose for my life feels the clearest? What part feels the most unclear?

4. What would it look like for me to take one small step toward alignment with God's blueprint today?

5. If my life were a constellation of purpose, which stars are burning brightest, and which ones need to be reignited?

Draw Your Constellation

Use the space below (or the next blank page) to sketch or list the key "stars" in your life right now (e.g., faith, family, talents, trials, victories). What story do they tell when connected? Is there a gap where a new star needs to rise?

Section 3

Beginning to Change

Believing that change is possible is powerful. But deciding to act on that belief is where transformation truly begins. In this section, we will explore how you can evaluate your life honestly, identify the "stars" that guide you, and start realigning your daily steps with God's purpose. These aren't just ideas—they're practical tools to help you make lasting, meaningful progress. This is the part where things start to shift. You've got what it takes. And you don't have to do it alone.

Chapter 6
Overcoming Obstacles and Adversities

The Bible is filled with narratives illustrating faith's triumph over adversity. Two notable examples are the story of Job and the Israelites' journey through the wilderness. These narratives offer profound insights into facing challenges, along with practical advice and strategies for overcoming setbacks.

Job's Story: Triumph through Perseverance and Faith

Job's narrative in the book bearing his name is a testament to unwavering faith in the face of extreme adversity. He endures the loss of his wealth, health, and family, yet he remains steadfast in his trust in God. The lesson from Job's story is that faith can triumph over even the most severe trials. In practical terms, this narrative teaches us the importance of patience, trust, and perseverance in the face of challenges.

The Israelites' Journey through the Wilderness: Resilience and Trust

The Israelites' journey from slavery in Egypt to the Promised Land involves numerous challenges, including hunger, thirst, and the uncertainty of the wilderness. Despite these difficulties, their faith in God sustains them. The biblical strategies include reliance on divine provision, trusting in God's guidance, and maintaining hope during challenging times.

Practical Advice and Biblical Strategies for Overcoming Challenges

Prayer and Seeking God's Guidance

Turn to prayer as a source of strength and guidance. Seek God's wisdom in navigating challenges, as exemplified by Solomon's prayer for wisdom:

> *At Gibeon the Lord appeared to Solomon during the night in a dream, and God said, "Ask for whatever you want me to give you." Solomon answered, "You have shown great kindness to your servant, my father David, because he was faithful to you and righteous and upright in heart. You have continued this great kindness to him and have given him a son to sit on his throne this very day.*
>
> *"Now, Lord my God, you have made your servant king in place of my father David. But I am only a little child and do not know how to carry out my duties. Your servant is here among the people you have chosen, a great people, too numerous to count or number. So give your servant a discerning heart to govern your people and*

to distinguish between right and wrong. For who is able to govern this great people of yours?"

The Lord was pleased that Solomon had asked for this. So God said to him, "Since you have asked for this and not for long life or wealth for yourself, nor have asked for the death of your enemies but for discernment in administering justice, I will do what you have asked. I will give you a wise and discerning heart, so that there will never have been anyone like you, nor will there ever be.

Moreover, I will give you what you have not asked for—both wealth and honor—so that in your lifetime you will have no equal among kings. And if you walk in obedience to me and keep my decrees and commands as David your father did, I will give you a long life."

—1 Kings 3:5–14

Community and Support

Connect with a supportive community. The Bible emphasizes the importance of fellowship and mutual support in overcoming challenges:

Two are better than one, because they have a good return for their labor: If either of them falls down, one can help the other up. But pity anyone who falls and has no one to help them up. Also, if two lie down together, they will keep warm. But how can one keep warm alone? Though one may be overpowered, two can defend themselves. A cord of three strands is not quickly broken.

—Ecclesiastes 4: 9–12

And let us consider how we may spur one another on toward love and good deeds, not giving up meeting together, as some are in the habit of doing, but encouraging one another—and all the more as you see the Day approaching.

—Hebrews 10: 24–25

Gratitude and Perspective

Cultivate gratitude even in challenging circumstances. The Apostle Paul's counsel in Philippians 4:6–7 encourages believers to approach challenges with thanksgiving, maintaining a positive perspective:

Do not be anxious about anything, but in every situation, by prayer and petition, with thanksgiving, present your requests to God. And the peace of God, which transcends all understanding, will guard your hearts and your minds in Christ Jesus.

Scripture and Meditation

Turn to the Bible for inspiration and guidance. Meditate on verses that provide strength and encouragement, such as Isaiah 41:10:

So do not fear, for I am with you; do not be dismayed, for I am your God. I will strengthen you and help you; I will uphold you with my righteous right hand.

And Philippians 4:13:

I can do all this through him who gives me strength.

Resilience and Endurance

Develop resilience and endurance. James 1:2–4 teaches that trials can produce perseverance and maturity in one's faith.

Consider it pure joy, my brothers and sisters, whenever you face trials of many kinds, because you know that the testing of your faith produces perseverance. Let perseverance finish its work so that you may be mature and complete, not lacking anything.

Personal Anecdotes

In 2023 and 2024, I faced one of my most significant transformational journeys when my wife and I separated and eventually divorced largely due to my past addiction and the hurts and damage that it—no, that I—had caused.

During that time, I encountered significant obstacles that tested my faith and resolve. I leaned heavily on prayer and sought the support of a close-knit community.

Reflecting on biblical narratives of triumph over adversity, I found solace in the idea that challenges are part of a larger narrative and that endurance leads to spiritual maturity. I came to understand that, as hard as my experience was, God could use it someday as a part of my story to help others.

While I am incredibly saddened by the death of my marriage, I know that doesn't define me, just as the addiction itself doesn't define who I am and who I'm going to be.

The practice of gratitude and maintaining a positive perspective, inspired by biblical teachings, played a crucial role in my overcoming setbacks. Turning to specific verses in times of doubt provided clarity and reassurance.

Embracing resilience, drawn from biblical principles and personal experiences, became a cornerstone of navigating challenges. Just as the Israelites endured the wilderness, recognizing that trials are part of the transformative journey helped me persevere.

These things got me through and kept me from turning to the addictions that I once thought provided me comfort and, in some ways, even a sense of security.

I continue to believe that even though I don't see the big picture being created, I'm serving the God who does. He will utilize everything I've gone through to benefit His Kingdom, providing ways for me to use it to help others.

In summary, biblical narratives and practical strategies emphasize the triumph of faith over adversity. Drawing on prayer, community, gratitude, Scripture, and resilience, we can navigate challenges with a purpose and ultimately experience transformation. My journey serves as a testament to the efficacy of these strategies in overcoming obstacles and finding strength in faith.

Closing Reflection: The Wilderness Is Not the End

Obstacles are not signs that you're on the wrong path; they're often proof that you're on a meaningful one. The Bible doesn't promise a life without trouble, but it *does* promise that we won't face it alone. Like Job, like the Israelites, like me, your story is still being written. That season of wilderness or loss may very well become the ground where your deepest roots of faith are planted.

If you're in the middle of something hard right now, don't assume that God has left you. The silence isn't absence; it may be preparation. Look back at how far you've come. Look at the prayers you've prayed that *have* been answered. Look at the strength you've gained from surviving what you thought would break you. You are not the same person you were, and that matters.

God's blueprint includes wildernesses and valleys, providing victory, healing, and restoration. Keep walking, keep praying, and keep trusting. The Promised Land is ahead.

A Prayer for Strength in the Storm

Father,

You see the battles I've fought—the ones I've fought out loud and the ones I've hid in the quiet. Thank You for never leaving my side, even when I doubted, even when I questioned, even when I broke.

Lord, help me remember that adversity does not mean abandonment. Strengthen my faith in the fire. Teach me to pray when I'm weak, to lean on others when I feel alone, and to lift my eyes when my head feels too heavy to hold up. Make me resilient—not because of my strength, but because of Yours.

Remind me that You are still working behind the scenes, even when I can't see it. Help me to be like Job, faithful through the pain; like the Israelites, learning to trust; and like Jesus, obedient, even when the road is hard.

Turn every obstacle into an opportunity to know You more deeply and reflect You more clearly. Let my scars tell a story of grace.

In Jesus's name,

Amen.

Journaling Challenge: Finding Strength in the Struggle

These journaling prompts will help you process past and current challenges, reflect on how God has been present in those moments, and recognize the growth that may have come from your most difficult seasons.

Take your time, be honest, and don't rush. These prompts are meant to help you *wrestle* and *rest* in God's faithfulness:

1. What is one obstacle in my life right now that feels overwhelming? How have I been trying to handle it on my own?

2. When have I experienced God's faithfulness in a past trial? What did He teach me through that season?

3. What do I need to surrender right now that I've been trying to control? What would it look like to fully trust God with it?

4. Who has been a source of strength for me during complex and challenging times? How might I intentionally invest in or express thanks in that relationship?

5. If I could speak to my past self in the middle of a storm, what encouragement would I offer? What do I now know that I didn't then?

6. What verse or story from Scripture brings me comfort in hard seasons? Why does it resonate with me?

7. What does resilience look like for me—not just surviving, but becoming stronger in my faith?

Chapter 7
Renewing Your Mind and Heart

After we overcome some of life's most complex trials, the next essential step is to renew our inner world, our thoughts, desires, and beliefs, so they reflect God's truth rather than our past pain.

Embarking on the transformative odyssey of renewing the mind and heart is an exhortation deeply etched in the sacred scrolls of biblical wisdom. The apostolic admonition from Romans 12:2 echoes with enduring resonance, urging believers not to conform to the fleeting patterns of this world but to undergo a transformative renewal of the mind. This transformative journey, intricately woven with prayer, meditation, and biblical study, constitutes a sacred dialogue and intentional alignment with divine truths.

Do not conform to the pattern of this world, but be transformed by the renewing of your mind. Then you will be able to test and approve what God's will is—his good, pleasing and perfect will.

—Romans 12:2

For you, this might look like setting aside ten minutes in the morning to read a psalm and journal a response, memorizing a verse each week to combat negative thoughts, or choosing to pause for prayer instead of reacting in frustration. Renewal isn't about perfection; it's about daily redirection.

Even if your renewal rhythm looks different each day—listening to Scripture in the car, praying during a walk, or journaling during lunch—what matters most is consistency, not perfection. The psalms are a poetic haven of spiritual introspection, particularly Psalm 1:2–3:

But whose delight is in the law of the Lord, and who meditates on his law day and night. That person is like a tree planted by streams of water, which yields its fruit in season and whose leaf does not wither— whatever they do prospers.

Meditation can be as simple as repeating a verse aloud while walking, writing it on a sticky note that you post by your mirror, or sitting quietly and asking God to speak through His Word. The goal isn't to master Scripture, but to let Scripture master us.

Scripture beckons believers to delight in the law of the Lord and meditate on it day and night. Meditation is not a passive act, but a dynamic engagement—a transformative practice that benefits the individual and serves as a conduit for profound transformation.

Meanwhile, 2 Timothy 3:16–17 articulates the indispensable role of biblical study, affirming that every Scripture is God-breathed, instructive for teaching, rebuking, correcting, and training in righteousness:

All Scripture is God-breathed and is useful for teaching, rebuking, correcting and training in righteousness, so that the servant of God may be thoroughly equipped for every good work.

These scriptural guideposts illuminate the transformative power encapsulated in the renewal process. Romans 12:2 unveils the promise that a renewed mind bestows the discernment required to fathom God's will, characterized by intrinsic goodness, undeniable pleasure, and unparalleled perfection. The verse reads:

Do not conform to the pattern of this world, but be transformed by the renewing of your mind. Then you will be able to test and approve what God's will is—his good, pleasing and perfect will.

Psalm 51:10, a poignant plea for a pure heart and a steadfast spirit, encapsulates the essence of this renewal. The verse reads: "*Create in me a pure heart, O God, and renew a steadfast spirit within me.*"

Ephesians 4:22–24, akin to a spiritual compass, instructs believers to shed the old self, embrace the renewal of their minds, and don a new self that is aligned with the righteousness and holiness of God:

You were taught, with regard to your former way of life, to put off your old self, which is being corrupted by its deceitful desires; to be made new in the attitude of your minds; and to put on the new self, created to be like God in true righteousness and holiness.

These scriptural precepts emerged as dependable companions in the crucible of my personal transformative journey. Through the conduit of prayer, I navigated uncharted depths, discovering a wellspring of strength and guidance beyond my understanding. The rhythmic practice of meditating on Scriptures became a transformative pilgrimage, allowing me to internalize and weave God's eternal truths into the very fabric of my thinking.

The ongoing process of biblical study, far from a mere intellectual exercise, has become a transformative guidepost, shaping my decision-making, fostering a deeper connection with my faith, and aligning the trajectory of my desires more closely with the eternal purposes outlined in God's Word.

Even Jesus modeled this kind of renewal. Though He was fully God, He continually withdrew to pray (Luke 5:16), sought solitude to align with the Father's will (Mark 1:35), and responded to temptation with Scripture (Matthew 4:1–11). His life shows us that a renewed mind isn't passive—it's practiced.

If Jesus used Scripture to fight lies and temptation, we can too. Write down a verse that counters a struggle you're facing, such as fear, shame, or anger, and keep the verse visible throughout your day.

The renewing of my mind was not a mere intellectual endeavor or a sporadic event; it became a deliberate, dynamic, and transformative process. Rather than being stumbling blocks, challenges metamorphosed into opportunities for profound growth.

Renewing your mind is not a one-time event; it's a daily, sometimes moment-by-moment, decision to choose God's truth over the lies you've believed. And like any meaningful transformation, it comes with ups and downs. Some days you'll feel strong and grounded; other times, you might feel like you've taken a step backward. That doesn't mean you've failed; it means you're still in the fight.

In recovery, it's often said that stumbles or setbacks are likely to occur, especially when you're just beginning your journey. But it's important not to fear those setbacks. Instead, take them as learning opportunities. In other words, it's okay to stumble in this journey of change, but make sure you're stumbling forward and not letting the stumbles hold you back.

Progress isn't always pretty, but it's still progress. What matters is that you continually return to the truth, realigning your thoughts with God's Word, and allowing Him to shape you from the inside out.

Setbacks are purposeful stepping stones on an upward ascent, and my heart's desires began to synchronize harmoniously with God's eternal purposes. The transformative journey of renewal, as exemplified in my life, underscores the profound impact of intentionally aligning thoughts and emotions with the timeless and transcendent truths encapsulated in the sacred pages of the Bible.

Closing Reflection: A Mind Made New

Transformation doesn't come by accident; it comes by intention. And the renewal of your mind and heart is not a one-time event but a daily invitation. When we fix our minds on what is true, noble, pure, lovely, and praiseworthy (Philippians 4:8), we begin to walk in the light of God's truth. We stop reacting from wounded places and start responding from a place of peace and wisdom. We become people who carry light in dark places—not because we're perfect, but because we've been renewed.

The more we meditate on God's Word, the more we begin to believe it. The more we believe it, the more we begin to live it. And over time, this changes not just how we think, but who we are.

So, what does renewal look like for you? Maybe it's replacing lies with truth. Perhaps it's learning to forgive. Possibly it's changing how you speak to yourself. Whatever it is, the invitation is clear: *"Be transformed."*

A Prayer for Renewal

Father,

Thank You for the invitation to renew my mind and heart through Your Word. I confess that sometimes my thoughts run wild, my fears speak louder than Your truth, and I fall into patterns that lead me away from You.

But today, I choose renewal. Renew my mind with Your wisdom. Replace anxiety with peace. Replace anger with gentleness. Replace insecurity with identity rooted in You.

Create in me a clean heart, O God. Help me hunger for Your truth more than the lies this world offers. Let Your Word take root in my soul so deeply that it changes how I think, speak, and live.

I don't want to be conformed—I want to be transformed.

Make me new, again and again.

In Jesus's name,

Amen.

Journaling Challenge: Thoughts That Transform

These journaling prompts will help you reflect on the thoughts and beliefs shaping your life and invite God to renew them:

1. What thought patterns or beliefs do I need to let go of in this season of my life?

2. What lies have I believed about myself, others, or God, and what does Scripture say instead?

3. How has my thinking changed as I've grown spiritually? What still needs renewing?

4. What verses from Scripture speak directly to the areas I struggle with most?

5. What would it look like to consistently *"take captive every thought"* (2 Corinthians 10:5) in my daily life?

6. How can I build a regular rhythm of meditation, prayer, and study to stay rooted in truth?

Chapter 8
Stepping into Your Transformed Future

As we embark on the journey of personal transformation, it's crucial to envision the lives we aspire to lead and set goals that resonate with our divine purpose. Envisioning our transformed selves allows us to craft a clear and compelling vision of the person we strive to become—a vision rooted in our deepest values, guided by faith, and aligned with our unique calling. Proverbs 16:3 says, *"Commit to the Lord whatever you do, and he will establish your plans."*

Take a moment to reflect deeply on what your ideal life looks like. What brings you joy, fulfillment, and a sense of purpose? Picture yourself embodying these qualities, aligning with your core values and beliefs. By painting a vivid mental image of our transformed lives, we set the stage for meaningful and purpose-driven goals.

Even Jesus lived with a clear sense of purpose. He often retreats to pray before making key decisions and reminds His followers that He came to do the will of the Father (John 6:38). His example reminds us that a life of purpose is both divine and deliberate.

With our vision in mind, it's time to translate it into actionable steps and set goals that propel us forward on our transformative journey. Begin by identifying specific areas where you seek growth and improvement, whether in your relationships, career, personal development, or spiritual life. Consider how each area aligns with your divine purpose and contributes to your overall vision of transformation. Then, break down your goals into smaller, measurable objectives that are both challenging and attainable.

For example, suppose one of your goals is to deepen your spiritual life. In that case, you might set objectives such as attending church regularly, engaging in daily prayer and meditation, or participating in a faith-based community or study group. By setting clear and actionable goals aligned with our divine purpose, we create a roadmap for our transformation journey and empower ourselves to take intentional steps toward realizing our vision.

Envisioning our transformed lives and setting goals aligned with our divine purpose are foundational to personal growth and fulfillment. As we embark on this journey, may we remain steadfast in our commitment to living authentically, guided by our deepest values and beliefs. And may our pursuit of transformation be fueled by faith, courage, and an unwavering belief in the boundless potential within each of us.

Taking concrete strides toward transformation in various areas of life involves committing to specific actions that propel us forward on our journey of personal growth and development.

Actionable Steps to Consider

Identify Areas for Growth

Reflect on different aspects of your life—such as relationships, career, health, and personal development—and identify areas where you seek improvement or transformation.

Set SMART Goals

Once you've identified areas for growth, set SMART (specific, measurable, achievable, relevant, time-bound) goals to guide your efforts. For example, if you want to improve your physical health, a SMART goal might be to exercise for thirty minutes five days a week for the next three months.

Create a Plan of Action

Break each goal into smaller, actionable steps that you can take to move closer to achieving the goal. This might involve researching resources, seeking support from others, or scheduling specific activities into your daily or weekly routine.

Take Consistent Action

Commit to taking consistent action toward your goals, even if progress feels slow or challenging at times. Consistency is key to long-term transformation.

Seek Support and Accountability

Enlist the support of friends, family members, mentors, or professionals who can offer encouragement, guidance, and hold you accountable as you work toward your goals.

Practice Self-Reflection

Reflect on your progress regularly and adjust your approach as needed. Celebrate your successes, learn from setbacks, and stay open to new insights and opportunities for growth.

Cultivate Positive Habits

Identify habits that support your goals and work on incorporating them into your daily routine. This might include mindfulness, gratitude, journaling, or regular self-care activities.

Stay Focused on Your Why

Remind yourself regularly why you're pursuing transformation in each area of your life. Keeping your motivations front and center can help you stay committed and inspired, especially during challenging times.

By taking actionable steps, you can make concrete strides toward transformation in various areas of your life. Remember that change is a gradual process, and each small step brings you closer to realizing your vision of a more fulfilling and purpose-driven life.

In conclusion, I invite you to act and commit to your transformational journey. Embrace the power within you to create positive change in your life and the lives of those around you. Take ownership of your growth and development, knowing that every step toward transformation brings you closer to living a life of purpose, fulfillment, and joy.

I challenge you to identify one area of your life where you're ready to experience growth and improvement. Set a SMART goal for yourself and create a plan of action to achieve it. Remember to stay consistent, seek support when needed, and celebrate your progress along the way.

Your transformational journey will not always be easy, but it will be worth it. Embrace the challenges as opportunities for growth, and keep your eyes focused on the vision of the person you aspire to become.

So, are you ready to embark on this journey of self-discovery and growth? Are you willing to step out of your comfort zone and embrace the possibilities that await you? I challenge you to take the first step today and commit to your transformational journey. Your future self will thank you for it.

A Prayer for Purpose and Bold Steps

Father,

Thank You for calling me into a life of purpose and transformation. You have given me a vision for who I can become and the strength to take steps toward it.

Give me courage when I feel uncertain, discipline when I'm tempted to quit, and faith to trust Your timing and path. Help me to walk boldly into the future, You have prepared for me, knowing that You go before me and walk beside me.

May my goals align with Your will. May my steps be steady and my spirit willing. May my transformation point others to You.

In Jesus's name,

Amen.

Journaling Challenge: My Next Right Step

1. What is one area of my life that feels ripe for transformation?

2. What is my "why" for pursuing growth in this area?

3. What SMART goal can I set today that aligns with God's purpose for my life?

4. Who can I ask to support and encourage me as I pursue this goal?

5. What Scripture will I cling to during this journey?

Conclusion

Since you've made it this far, I want you to know that your journey matters. Transformation isn't just possible; it's already unfolding. It doesn't happen in a single moment, but in the consistent steps you've taken to seek something more.

Significant change is not achieved through a singular event but through consistent and intentional effort. Remember that the path to transformation is paved with challenges and setbacks, each presenting an opportunity for learning and personal development. By embracing these obstacles as part of the process, you can cultivate resilience and perseverance, essential qualities for navigating the ups and downs of life's journey.

Set clear goals aligned with your vision for transformation and take actionable steps toward achieving them. This approach emphasizes the importance of staying committed to these goals, even when progress feels slow or difficult. Through consistent action and dedication, you can gradually move closer to realizing your aspirations and becoming the person you aspire to be.

Moreover, seeking support and guidance from others is also very important. As the saying goes, "life is better connected."

Surrounding yourself with a supportive community can provide invaluable assistance and encouragement on the transformative journey, whether through the wisdom of mentors, the encouragement of friends and family, or the expertise of professionals. However, you must also take time for self-reflection to gauge progress, celebrate successes, and learn from setbacks.

Furthermore, you must remain open to change and embrace new opportunities for growth and self-improvement. By cultivating a mindset of curiosity and openness, you can continue to evolve and adapt to life's ever-changing circumstances.

Ultimately, only you can choose to change your stars. God has equipped you, but it's up to you to take the first step. Remember that transformation is not a destination to reach but a continuous process to embrace—a journey of self-discovery, growth, and becoming.

I continue to be active in my church and Celebrate Recovery. My relationship with Jesus grows stronger each day as I learn to pray more frequently, and I'm developing the habit of spending time in the Word daily.

Since starting my recovery journey, I've gone through a couple of step studies. For those unfamiliar with CR, a step study is an in-depth dive through the twelve steps of recovery while focusing on a specific area of your life.

Through these studies, I have dug deeper into what makes me who I am today. I've developed relationships with groups of men that I can honestly say will last a lifetime. I know that wherever life takes me, I have a group of guys I can call on and be honest with, and they can be honest with me in return.

Remember, God is in your corner, no matter where you are in your faith or life journey, even if it feels like no one else is. He's not finished with you. He loves you and is there for you. Sometimes, the life lessons we are forced to learn are hard. However, as we've seen throughout this book, even biblical characters struggled with their life journeys. But the hard times and experiences we've faced are what make us and our stories unique!

I encourage you to lean on your faith as a source of strength, guidance, and unwavering support, just as I've had to many times. Regardless of your religious background or spiritual beliefs, faith can serve as a powerful anchor during life's uncertainties. It provides a sense of purpose and meaning, reminding us that we are part of something greater than ourselves.

Embrace your unique path of change, recognizing that your journey is unlike anyone else's. Everyone is on their trajectory of growth and discovery, shaped by their experiences, values, and aspirations. Trust in the process, knowing that every step you take, no matter how small, leads you closer to becoming the person you are meant to be.

Embrace your faith as a guiding light, illuminating the path ahead and providing clarity in moments of doubt or confusion. Draw strength from the teachings and principles that resonate with your heart, allowing them to inform your decisions and actions as you navigate the challenges and triumphs of transformation.

Remember that your faith is not a static entity but a dynamic force that evolves and deepens over time. Lean into the wisdom of spiritual mentors, seek solace in prayer and meditation, and remain open to the insights and revelations from divine guidance.

Above all, trust in the journey and believe in the transformative power within you. Embrace your faith as a companion on the path of change, guiding you toward a future filled with purpose, fulfillment, and abundant blessings. As you embark on this journey, may your faith be a constant source of comfort, courage, and unwavering hope, propelling you forward with confidence and grace.

As I reflect on my transformational journey, I am filled with gratitude for the profound impact it has had on my life. It has been a journey of self-discovery, growth, and spiritual awakening, marked by challenges and triumphs, setbacks, and successes.

Through the transformational process, I have learned to embrace my vulnerabilities and imperfections, recognizing them as opportunities for growth rather than obstacles to overcome. I have discovered the strength and resilience within me, tapping into reservoirs of courage and determination I never knew I possessed.

Even though it is a work in progress, my transformation has deepened my faith and strengthened my connection to something/someone greater than myself. It has taught me to trust in God's timing and surrender to the unfolding of life's mysteries, knowing that everything happens for a reason and that every experience has a purpose.

Perhaps most importantly, my transformation journey has taught me the power of authenticity and self-love. I have cultivated a sense of inner peace and acceptance that transcends external circumstances by embracing my true self, flaws and all. I have learned to love myself unconditionally, recognizing that true happiness comes from within and cannot be found in the approval of others or the pursuit of external achievements.

As I continue my transformation journey, I am filled with excitement for the possibilities. I know that the road may be long and challenging at times, but I am confident that as long as I stay true to myself and remain open to the guidance of my faith, I will continue to evolve and grow into the best version of myself.

The bottom line is that it is possible to change your stars. You can go from desperation, addiction, or a life of crime to royalty, a son or daughter of King Jesus, and He can use your story to help others!

May your transformation journey serve as a beacon of hope and inspiration for others, reminding them that no matter where they are on their path, they can transform their lives and create a future filled with purpose, fulfillment, and joy.

Remember, there is nothing that God can't overcome if you will only trust Him to help you.

You can change your stars and go from peasant to royalty like the boy in the movie mentioned at the start of this book. When you trust in God, put your faith in Him, and accept Him as your Savior, you shed your peasant clothing and become a part of a royal family.

Now go, change your stars, walk boldly in your purpose, and never forget that you are seen, you are loved, you are called, and you are capable of anything through and with Christ Jesus.

Final Blessings

May you walk forward with courage, knowing that your past does not define you, God does.

May every step you take be guided by divine purpose, and every setback be seen as soil for growth.

May your heart remain open to change, your mind renewed by truth, and your spirit anchored in grace.

May the stars of your life shine brightly—not because they are perfect, but because they reflect the light of the One who called you.

And may you never forget:

> You are seen.
> You are loved.
> You are chosen.

You are being transformed, day by day, moment by moment.

Now go, live boldly, love deeply, and change your stars.

Amen.

Epilogue: Becoming Never Ends

I want to pause and say thank you, from the bottom of my heart, not just for reading this book, but for choosing to engage with your own story. That takes courage. It takes humility. And it takes faith.

Throughout *The Blueprint of Becoming*, I've been honest with you, and I hope that you've been just as honest with yourself. We've explored some hard truths about addiction, shame, pain, identity, and healing. We've also examined the hope found in Scripture, personal testimony, and the power of surrender. But if there's one thing, I want you to take with you, it's this: Becoming is a lifelong process.

There's no moment when you arrive at perfection. But there are plenty of moments when you become more aligned with who God created you to be. Moments when you choose grace over guilt, truth over lies, healing over hiding. Moments when you take one more faithful step.

Your past? It doesn't disqualify you.

Your pain? It can be used.

Your doubts? They don't scare God.

No matter where you are, the blueprint God designed for your life is still intact. It's never too late to build something beautiful—one prayer, one decision, one surrendered step at a time.

So, keep going.

Keep showing up in your life.

Keep leaning into God's presence.

Keep becoming, because your story isn't over.

And when you find yourself on solid ground again, don't forget to turn around and help someone else take their first step. That's how we grow. That's how we heal. That's how we walk out the blueprint together.

With you in the journey,
Wesley Farnsworth

Scripture Index

Introduction

- Psalm 139:14 – *"I praise you because I am fearfully and wonderfully made; your works are wonderful, I know that full well."*
- Jeremiah 1:5 – *"Before I formed you in the womb I knew you, before you were born I set you apart; I appointed you as a prophet to the nations."*

Chapter 1: Roots and Wings

- Philippians 4:19 – *"And my God will meet all your needs according to the riches of his glory in Christ Jesus."*
- Colossians 3:13 – *"Bear with each other and forgive one another if any of you has a grievance against someone. Forgive as the Lord forgave you"*

Chapter 2: Breaking Chains

- No specific Scripture citations, but the chapter contains multiple biblical allusions and CR step references.

Chapter 3: The Power of Transformation in the Bible

- Ezekiel 36:26 – *"I will give you a new heart and put a new spirit in you; I will remove from you your heart of stone and give you a heart of flesh."*

- John 3:3–5 – *"Jesus replied, "Very truly I tell you, no one can see the kingdom of God unless they are born again."*

  "How can someone be born when they are old?" Nicodemus asked. "Surely they cannot enter a second time into their mother's womb to be born!"

  Jesus answered, "Very truly I tell you, no one can enter the kingdom of God unless they are born of water and the Spirit."

- 2 Corinthians 4:16-18 – *"Therefore, we do not lose heart. Though outwardly we are wasting away, yet inwardly we are being renewed day by day. For our light and momentary troubles are achieving for us an eternal glory that far outweighs them all. So, we fix our eyes not on what is seen, but on what is unseen, since what is seen is temporary, but what is unseen is eternal."*

- Romans 3:23 – *"for all have sinned and fall short of the glory of God."*

- 2 Corinthians 10:3 – "For though we live in the world, we do not wage war as the world does."

Chapter 4: Understanding Your Current Stars

- Psalm 147:4 – "He determines the number of the stars and calls them each by name."

Scripture Index

Chapter 5: The Divine Blueprint

- Jeremiah 29:11 – *"For I know the plans I have for you," declares the Lord, "plans to prosper you and not to harm you, plans to give you hope and a future."*

- Proverbs 3:5–6 – *"Trust in the Lord with all your heart and lean not on your own understanding; in all your ways submit to him, and he will make your paths straight."*

- Psalm 37:23 – *"The Lord makes firm the steps of the one who delights in him."*

- Ephesians 2:10 – *"For we are God's handiwork, created in Christ Jesus to do good works, which God prepared in advance for us to do"*

- Romans 12:2 – *"Do not conform to the pattern of this world, but be transformed by the renewing of your mind. Then you will be able to test and approve what God's will is—his good, pleasing and perfect will."*

- Psalm 139:16 – *"Your eyes saw my unformed body; all the days ordained for me were written in your book before one of them came to be"*

Chapter 6: Overcoming Obstacles and Adversities

- 1 Kings 3:5–14 – *" Moreover, I will give you what you have not asked for—both wealth and honor—so that in your lifetime you will have no equal among kings. And if you walk in obedience to me and keep my decrees and commands as David your father did, I will give you a long life."*

- Ecclesiastes 4:9–12 – *"Two are better than one, because they have a good return for their labor: If either of them falls down,* one can help the other up. But pity anyone who falls and has no one to help them up. Also, if two lie down together, they will keep warm. But how can one keep warm alone? Though one may be overpowered, two can defend themselves. A cord of three strands is not quickly broken."

- Hebrews 10:24–25 – *"And let us consider how we may spur one another on toward love and good deeds, not giving up meeting together, as some are in the habit of doing, but encouraging one another—and all the more as you see the Day approaching."*

- Philippians 4:6–7 – *"Do not be anxious about anything, but in every situation, by prayer and petition, with thanksgiving, present your requests to God. And the peace of God, which transcends all understanding, will guard your hearts and your minds in Christ Jesus."*

- Isaiah 41:10 – *"So do not fear, for I am with you; do not be dismayed, for I am your God. I will strengthen you and help you; I will uphold you with my righteous right hand."*

- Philippians 4:13 – *"I can do all this through him who gives me strength."*

- James 1:2–4 – *"Consider it pure joy, my brothers and sisters, whenever you face trials of many kinds, because you know that the testing of your faith produces perseverance. Let perseverance finish its work so that you may be mature and complete, not lacking anything."*

Chapter 7: Renewing Your Mind and Heart

- Romans 12:2 – *"Do not conform to the pattern of this world, but be transformed by the renewing of your mind. Then you will be able to test and approve what God's will is—his good, pleasing and perfect will."*

- Psalm 1:2–3 – *" But whose delight is in the law of the Lord, and who meditates on his law day and night. That person is like a tree planted by streams of water, which yields its fruit in season and whose leaf does not wither— whatever they do prospers."*

- Psalm 51:10 – *"Create in me a pure heart, O God, and renew a steadfast spirit within me."*

- Ephesians 4:22–24 – *"You were taught, with regard to your former way of life, to put off your old self, which is being corrupted by its deceitful desires; to be made new in the attitude of your minds; and to put on the new self, created to be like God in true righteousness and holiness."*

- 2 Timothy 3:16–17 – *"All Scripture is God-breathed and is useful for teaching, rebuking, correcting and training in righteousness, so that the servant of God may be thoroughly equipped for every good work."*

- Philippians 4:8 – "Finally, brothers and sisters, whatever is true, whatever is noble, whatever is right, whatever is pure, whatever is lovely, whatever is admirable–if anything is excellent or praiseworthy–think about such things.

- 2 Corinthians 10:5 – "We demolish arguments and every pretension that sets itself up against the knowledge of god, and we take captive every thought to make it obedient to Christ."

Chapter 8: Stepping into Your Transformed Future

- Proverbs 16:3 – *"Commit to the Lord whatever you do, and he will establish your plans."*
- John 6:38 – "For I have come down from heaven not to do my will but to do the will of him who sent me."

Scripture Reference Table by Topic

Identity and Purpose

- Psalm 139:14
- Jeremiah 1:5
- Ephesians 2:10
- Psalm 139:16
- Proverbs 16:9
- John 6:38

Transformation and Renewal

- Romans 12:2
- Psalm 51:10
- Ephesians 4:22–24
- 2 Timothy 3:16–17
- Psalm 1:2–3
- 2 Corinthians 10:5
- Philippians 4:8

Overcoming Trials and Perseverance

- Job (entire book)
- James 1:2–4
- Isaiah 41:10
- Philippians 4:13
- Philippians 4:6–7
- 1 Kings 3:5–14

Faith and Trust

- Proverbs 3:5–6
- Psalm 37:23
- Romans 3:23
- Ecclesiastes 4:9–12
- Hebrews 10:24–25

Forgiveness and Grace

- Colossians 3:13
- Luke 15 (prodigal son)
- Genesis 50:20 (Joseph's story)

Action and Growth

- Proverbs 16:3
- 2 Corinthians 4:16-18
- Jeremiah 29:11

About the Author

For much of my life, I lived a story I didn't fully understand. On the outside, I looked like I had it together—a pastor's kid who knew the Scriptures and said the right things. But beneath the surface, I was hiding. I struggled with shame, addiction, co-dependency, anger, and the constant fear that I wasn't enough. It wasn't until my marriage hit a breaking point that I stopped pretending and finally confronted my brokenness.

That season marked the beginning of true transformation. Through counseling, confession, community, and grace, I began to heal and discover who God created me to be. *The Blueprint of Becoming* is the result. It's not just a book, but a companion for anyone who feels stuck between who they are and who they're called to be. In *The Blueprint of Becoming*, you'll find real stories, biblical truth, and practical tools for lasting change.

Professionally, I've spent over sixteen years as a photographer and storyteller, both in the US Air Force and the private sector. I also hold two master's degrees in branding and internet marketing, and I now use that experience to help others communicate with clarity and purpose.

Today, I'm actively involved in Celebrate Recovery and am available to speak at churches, men's retreats, and recovery events. My mission is simple: to help others discover their God-given blueprint and walk it out. If you feel too far gone or too broken, let me assure you, you're not. You're precisely the kind of person God loves to redeem.

Let's walk this journey together.

Additional Resources

Your journey doesn't have to end with the final chapter. *The Blueprint of Becoming* was designed to be more than a book—it's an invitation to take your next steps with intention, clarity, and support.

Explore these free tools and resources to continue growing:

- **Find Your Starting Point: Take the Quiz.** Not sure where to begin? The Blueprint Assessment Quiz will help you identify what area of your life may need the most attention right now.

    Discover your current stage of transformation.
    Get a personalized description and practical suggestions.
    Take your next step with confidence.

- **Lead Others on the Journey: Small Group Leader's Guide.** Interested in bringing *The Blueprint of Becoming* to your church, recovery group, or small group?

    Download the free 10-week Leader's Guide, which includes:
    * Weekly discussion questions
    * Scripture references

* Prayers and reflection prompts
* Leadership tips and group facilitation help

- More tools are coming soon. I'm building a library of additional resources to support your transformation.

Explore these additional tools and resources, or request Wesley to speak at your church, event, or group at: https://www.blueprintofbecoming.com.

www.ingramcontent.com/pod-product-compliance
Lightning Source LLC
Chambersburg PA
CBHW070503100426
42743CB00010B/1747